Touching Creatures,
Touching Spirit

Touching Creatures, Touching Spirit

LIVING IN A SENTIENT WORLD

stories & essays

JUDY GRAHN

Red Hen Press | *Pasadena, CA*

Book design by Mark E. Cull

Library of Congress Cataloging-in-Publication Data

Names: Grahn, Judy, 1940– author.
Title: Touching creatures, touching spirit : living in a sentient world :
   stories & essays / Judy Grahn.
Description: First edition. | Pasadena, CA : Red Hen Press, [2021]
Identifiers: LCCN 2020050218 (print) | LCCN 2020050219 (ebook) | ISBN
   9781597091183 (trade paperback) | ISBN 9781597098816 (epub)
Subjects: LCSH: Panpsychism. | Consciousness.
Classification: LCC BD560 .G73 2021 (print) | LCC BD560 (ebook) | DDC
   141—dc23
LC record available at https://lccn.loc.gov/2020050218
LC ebook record available at https://lccn.loc.gov/2020050219

The National Endowment for the Arts, the Los Angeles County Arts Commission, the Ahmanson Foundation, the Dwight Stuart Youth Fund, the Max Factor Family Foundation, the Pasadena Tournament of Roses Foundation, the Pasadena Arts & Culture Commission and the City of Pasadena Cultural Affairs Division, the City of Los Angeles Department of Cultural Affairs, the Audrey & Sydney Irmas Charitable Foundation, the Kinder Morgan Foundation, the Meta & George Rosenberg Foundation, the Albert and Elaine Borchard Foundation, the Adams Family Foundation, the Riordan Foundation, Amazon Literary Partnership, the Sam Francis Foundation, and the Mara W. Breech Foundation partially support Red Hen Press.

First Edition
Published by Red Hen Press
www.redhen.org

Acknowledgments

Thanks to editors of the following publications where these stories appeared: *Dark Matter*: "Dragonfly Dances"; *Spoon Knife 3: Incursions*: "Only Strawberries Don't Have Fathers"; *Strange Attractors*: "Messages with Cats Attached" first published as "Fractal Cats"; *Zyzzyva*: "Rats at the Door of Love."

So much gratitude for:

Moral support, research, and invaluable feedback, as well as editing: Kris Brandenburger, Dianne E. Jenett, Dawn McGuire, Dorothy Ettling, Margaret Grove, Martha Shelley, Anne Carol Mitchell, D'vorah Grenn, Brynn Saito, Coletta Reid, Anne Huffman, Angela Hume.

People who show up in the stories, one way or another, or who told me their stories, or who saw me through some phase: Dianne E. Jenett, Kris Brandenburger, Ruth Rhoten, Rachel deVries, Alice Molloy, Carol Wilson, Susan Abbott, Betty De Shong Meador, Vera Grahn, Elmer Grahn, Rodney Grahn, Eloise Klein Healy, Dawn McGuire, Ellie Armer, Ed May, Jack Foley, Paula Gunn Allen, Peggy Lauer, Wendyn Cadden, Katarzyna Rolzinski, Elinor Gadon and eleven women in her PhD cohort, Luisah Teish, Quin Delamer, Toi Derricotte, Tina Frisco, Willyce Kim, Bhagwan Shri Rajneesh.

Invaluable editors who published pieces: Lise Weil, Howard Junker, Nick Walker, Edie Meidav.

Marvelous publishers, Kate Gale, Mark Cull, Tobi Harper of Red Hen Press and their wonderful staff, especially Natasha McClellan, Monica Fernandez, Ryan Taylor Brideau, and Rebeccah Sanhueza.

To my parents,
Vera Doris Grahn and Elmer August Grahn
And to Sister Dorothy Ettling

Contents

Introduction
by Jenny Factor

Judy Grahn's *Touching Creatures, Touching Spirit* is sly and savvy activism couched in other terms. To read *Touching Creatures, Touching Spirit* is to remember that we live less in the world of animals as intimates and more the world of animal as internet meme. Like the works of ecofeminism from which Critical Animal Studies and Human Animal Studies claim root, Grahn's theory is ready-made to be put into practice. Grahn's *Touching Creatures, Touching Spirit* is about capturing a world—our whole interconnected, living world—before it has slipped out of our consciousness and into realms beyond our possible reclamation.

Touching Creatures, Touching Spirit is a genre-expanding work. The philosophies and comedies energizing Grahn's book are essentially questions of communication in relationships. Yet in addition to friends and lovers, Grahn's characters are ideas, cats, dark shapes, dragonflies, gut microbes, even cells that are "inherited." Her book insists that the writer unfailingly slip outside a reductive "I" to configure a "we." Grahn asks, "When I say 'my body,' whose body am I talking about?" Gesturing to the small acquired and native life forms that collectively animate us, Grahn concludes, "At the cellular level, 'our body' or even 'our bodies' is more accurate." Martin Buber once famously pronounced that all true life is "meeting." That Grahn is able to achieve a strong sense of meeting with her nonhuman characters is part of why this book may be read as a milestone for both feminism and humanism. With Grahn serving as we-diviner and spiritual mythmaker, the book's very title points, with its triad of gerunds ("touching," "touching," "living"), toward the mystery of sentient connection, a radiant collection of warmth, wisdom, alternate epistemologies, and fresh modes of love.

In "Intimate Familiarities? Feminism and Human Animal Studies," Lynda Birke echoes Joan Dunayer when she notes that "women have long been denigrated by animal epithets" and adds that these are "mostly loaded with loathing." She continues, "The study of human-nonhuman animal relationships [is] like women's studies . . . [expressing a] belief that politics that ignore other oppressions cannot be liberatory politics for anyone." She concludes that the link between woman and animal is still urgent, "If nonhuman animals are outside modern feminist theory, it is partly because of the way that women and animals are linked as 'others'." This alliance of others has ever been one of Grahn's principle topics.

During her sixty-year career in arts and activism, Grahn has stood as a lightning rod for the cause of intersectionality, at times proving a catalyst toward creating a more inclusive women's movement. Her 1971 book, *Edward the Dyke and Other Poems*, pioneered the reappropriation of oppressive nomenclature and pushed to bring nonnormative genders and nonbinarism into the center of the ideologies of 1970s liberation. Her first memoir, *A Simple Revolution: The Making of an Activist Poet*, eschews individual memory ("that oozy and changeable bog") in favor of an interview-and-inclusion technique. "It seemed . . . arrogant to try to tell a group story using only my own limited memory," Grahn writes in that memoir's introduction. Grahn's working-class, common woman "I" has always included Whitmanesque multitudes, paired with a commitment to empathy as truth. Yet while Grahn penned, in her 1974 "A Woman Is Talking to Death" a tapestried epic of radical empathic generosity, here in *Touching Creatures, Touching Spirit*, Grahn at last makes explicit her belief that humanist work ultimately must include nonhuman sentience in our net of connections. "Bless this day oh cat our house," is a refrain in "A Woman Is Talking to Death;" but in *Touching Creatures, Touching Spirit*, Grahn *demonstrates* how daily alertness to creature consciousness is required for our eyes to be honest, our self-other constructions to be true.

Meanwhile, we move through fields where the bees' voices are silenced, the ant is exiled, and the common animals of our childhood are facing imminent extinctions. Might not Grahn's work lead us to question the necropolitics of biocapital and take "a stance against" what Nik Taylor and Richard Twine term "an anthropocentric status quo"? In *When Species Meet*, biologist and theorist Donna Haraway argues for what activists call an "alter-globalization"—an anticapitalist, posthuman way of experiencing ourselves in a global world: "My interest is in how to process the encounters with creature consciousness, involving intentional interactions and communications from nonhuman beings . . ." Haraway's work reminds me of Grahn's. Like the academic context of Haraway the biologist, Grahn's early experiences as both "medical laboratory technician and as a student of sociology" give her thinking white masculinist bona fides. Yet Grahn explains the equally resonant power of "Poetic License"—a practice that gives artists working with the unclaimed potencies of other genre and media (in fact, genres such as the frictive or fictive stories in this book), the ability to use epistemologies not grounded already in heterosexist, racialized, oppressive norms. "[D]iverse bodies and meanings coshape one another," Donna Haraway declares in a book that predicts Grahn's own work's importance. When "dimensions tangle," Haraway tells us, they "require response." Grahn's *Touching Creatures, Touching Spirit* is exactly such a response. We are all, Haraway reminds us, implicated by the many ways "ordinary knotted beings gather up those who respond to them into unpredictable kinds of 'we'."

It is this unpredictable configuration of "we" that has always been Grahn's most beautiful gift to us. She finds in the "we" the very life force that counteracts the tendency of inanimate structures to replicate the machineries of death. By reading along, we discover in this collection not only Judy Grahn. We may find a way of opening our eyes to our unceasing silent communications with manifestations of the earth's spirit. We may find ourselves and learn why we are all still needed, leaning in, human and animal, mineral and biome, listening hard, locating one another, while there's still time.

Cambridge, MA
August 20, 2020

Preface
Frameworks

We must begin really to listen to the rest of life.
—Lynn Margulis and Dorion Sagan, *What Is Life?*

On those amazing occasions when creatures reach across to us, how do we interpret what this means? How could we show that wild creatures as well as our companion animals are responsive to us, and reach out at times? One way is to describe incidents of intervention that seem beyond coincidental. Creatures who intersect with us at momentous times of our lives, creatures who do unexpected things. Like the Siamese fighting fish beloved of poet Toi Derricotte, who, once as she leaned over the bowl, leaped straight up out of the water and kissed her on the lips, described in her poem, "For Telly the Fish." Or the two dozen little river fish in my thirty-gallon tank who greeted me after a three-month absence by crowding to the end of the tank close to my chair and looking at me. They always stayed in their own family groups and in specific parts of the tank. I had never seen them act like this, all bunched together, facing me for several minutes in what I know to read only as a one-time act of recognition and greeting.

By now enough of us have seen adorable videos online of Jasmine, a rescued greyhound adopting a dozen varied orphans at the shelter, including a fawn and an owl. We've seen the rabbit snuggling up to the tortoise, and the dog muzzle to snout with the porpoise or muzzle to beak with the duck. We've laughed over the crow and kitten playmates rolling on their backs as they wrestle in a meadow. We've been moved by the video of a mother lion protecting the injured fox as if it were her cub, and of Odin the Great Pyrenees dog insisting on staying with his flock of goats, guiding them through the horrific Sonoma County fire that devastated his neighborhood. We get it that creatures are empathetic across species.

Most of us have ample examples of having rescued creatures, or knowing someone who did, or at least seeing one of hundreds of videos: fishermen cutting a whale loose from lines; a hiker pulling a bear cub out of flood water; workers digging a dog out of the drain pipe, and on and on. Occasionally we hear a story of a creature rescuing one of us, dogs giving an alarm usually. A less usual example was told by one of my students who swam too far out in a lake and became confused and nearly drowned, until a dragonfly arrived and very clearly led the way to shore.

My interest is in how to process the encounters with creature consciousness, involving intentional interactions and communications from nonhuman beings, as well as encounters with that even more mysterious aspect we call spirit. Such singular events have happened to me or have been experienced by friends. What significant part do they play in our lives? What do these events imply about the world in which we live? What greater understandings do they impart? How do we talk about them?

My education in the early 1960s both as a medical laboratory technician and as a student of sociology had tried to teach me to be indifferent to the lives of nonhuman beings, to think of them as lesser beings with short, brutal lives, mysteriously driven by "instinct" and not by emotion, connection, culture, family. I was instructed to think of them as needing to fulfill some human need in order to matter; or simply not to think of them at all. As I struggled to maintain the limitless curiosity of my childhood, repeatedly awakened to a consciousness of their consciousness, the later 1960s concept of the "oneness of the universe" did not help me. I was expected to live in the world of "man alone": as the lonely individuated human who, at most, looks throughout the cosmos for other planets with possible beings with a consciousness like mine. The alternative to this seemed to be an expectation that I might (occasionally), in an altered state, sense a connection with "everything," but, in those moments, not to anything or anyone in particular. Yet, it has been in my close observations and interactions with *particular* beings in nature that I have learned the most about them and their varieties of consciousness in interaction with my own. This is a book about that particularity: our experiences with beings who live close to us, in our houses, yards, neighborhoods or nearby land; even those within our bodies.

Deciding to write stories, and needing some interesting impetus to really do it, I gave myself the assignment that every story should feature interactions with a creature or other-than-human being, recounted 100 percent as experienced. The experience must be witnessed by others if possible and must shape the central axis of the story. Even if I needed to disguise, slightly, some of the human characters, as I've done in all four of the creative nonfiction stories, for the sake of confidentiality, anecdotes of encounters with spirit and creature must be accurately described and true. Some of what I was writing evolved into an essay format, which I call "accounts," to distinguish from the slightly fictionalized "stories. "

In trying really to see our fellow creatures, I have tried not to think of them as "cute," like a fantasy grandchild. I have tried to know them as members of their own families, even including those who are family to me. Along the way I have had to learn to try not to objectify. I've left most of my painful failures with creatures out of the stories, thinking we have enough sorrow with the crises that other creatures as well as humans are enduring from human-caused climate change. We need, or at least I need, to concentrate on how better to communicate with and comprehend nonhuman beings. And the more closely I examined instances of intraspecies "reaching across" in my own and friends' lives, the more curious I have become about how they might fit in an overall scheme of "the real." This includes the possibility of a greater net of *mind* enfolding all of us, not easily explained. Four of the stories center on how our fantasies and projections of human imagination can distort any understanding of our fellow beings, while the other accounts describe instances of what is called "paranormal" and "extrasensory," and, more recently, "parapsychological," and "transpersonal" experiences, including messages delivered by creatures through dreams and other methods. These experiences have made a psychic connection between human and nonhuman consciousness impossible to deny.

I have felt a need to engage the full range of my life experience, sorting through various transpersonal events in my life and seeking a vocabulary for them. I have needed to distinguish between what has been real, though puzzling, and what has been imaginary, or wishful. After tracking the paranormal presences in my own life, I am struck by the range. Creatures, even insects, have reached out to connect with me in unusual ways: mind-reading cats; a coyote grieving the death of a woman who had lived in its territory; love falling out of the sky; birds crashing out of their lives and into mine as I work on a particular story about birds; and more.

To indigenous knowledges I owe specific examples of the interplay of consciousness among all beings. I became more aware of this consciousness, in understanding that a creation goddess can be a spider (Keres people, Paula Gunn Allen, personal communication) or in India, can take the form of a cockroach beetle (Ritualist Mahalakshmi Gangadharan on goddess Mariamma, personal communication), or that a bird can show up to participate in a human ritual (Bharani Festival, in South India, personal observation), or that a lizard's croak can be understood to affirm the truth or falsity of a human conversation (the Princess Gouri Lakshmi Bayi of Thiruvananthapuram, personal observation). These examples taught or confirmed my earliest understanding of the permeability of all life forms to rays or waves of consciousness between beings.

Which theories of consciousness, which philosophical positions, come close to making room for the interconnected world many of us have experienced? The venerable William James expressed the idea of individual consciousness as similar to a magnetic field. Carl Jung named paranormally related events "synchronicities." Theories and data from experiments by a number of scientists and philosophers have helped me frame what I have gathered.

Aldous Huxley popularized the idea that we live within an "ocean of consciousness," from which we can gather knowledge, and which can move the mind way beyond its little cage of skull. Transpersonal studies spun this ocean into a full-blown field beginning in the 1960s, when a generation of American youth experimented with "mind-expanding drugs" that led to descriptions of altered states characterized by a powerful sense of oneness with all creation. Drugs did not lead me, personally, in this direction—none of my stories has anything to do with drugs—yet the field of transpersonal psychology has provided a basis for redefining altered states as part of the potential of human life, rather than as pathological or legitimated only in relation to an organized mystical tradition. Glenn Hartelius, scholar and professor of transpersonal psychology and Jorge Ferrer, professor of psychology and religion, turn from a religiously based idea that all experiences of ecstatic awe, for example, require for legitimacy a relationship to a singular, omniscient, creator "above." Rather, as Ferrer says, consciousness is "an ocean with many beaches," making the paths to ecstatic or psychic experiences multiple, and horizontal, and specific.

My mother experienced visions, some of them predictive, some hallucinatory. She was terrified to speak of them, lest she be locked in a mental ward and subjected to mind-altering procedures, to say nothing of being ostracized by her family and community. In my lifetime, some attitudes have been changing, although scorn for those of us who experience and want to talk about the "paranormal" in our lives is not uncommon. This causes us to remain cautious about how and with whom to share stories, if somewhat less terrified of being locked away.

Science and philosophy are by no means in lockstep over just what "mind" is, and how it receives information, and good-faith arguments allow for an expansion of credible viewpoints. Transpersonal studies have helped legitimize a broad range of parapsychological experience, while the new field of neurodiversity, which describes humans as having natural divergences of perception and neurological "wiring," is lending credibility to ancient modes of perception and helping redefine what had been dismissed as pathology or even insanity. Some ecologists are looking to partner with animists, those who attribute a soul to plants and nonhuman beings, recognizing that old wisdom offers something missing from mass culture.

Fredrik Ullén, a professor of cognitive neuroscience at the prestigious Karolinka Institute in Stockholm, has expanded on the idea of consciousness as a vast surround, and of the brain organizing its input, in relation to both those with a high degree of creativity and also those with schizophrenia.

Ullén and colleagues looked at the brain's dopamine (D2) receptor genes which experts believe govern divergent thought. He found that highly creative people who did well on tests for divergence of thought had a lower than expected density of D2 receptors in the thalamus—as do people with schizophrenia. The thalamus serves as a relay centre, filtering information before it reaches areas of the cortex, which is responsible for, amongst other things, cognition and reasoning. The brains of schizophrenics have less gray matter and fewer synaptic connections, but more unmediated mental contents. Huxley's "filter" theory of consciousness is relevant here. As the novelist Michael Prescott summarizes, "the filter theory . . . sees the brain as a kind of reducing valve for consciousness. There is a vast ocean of higher consciousness and then there is a far more limited consciousness available to us for our physical, earthly existence. The brain's function is not to originate consciousness but to filter it to us in small, manageable quantities. A corollary to this is that less brain function should in some cases lead to more consciousness." Schizophrenics may, in fact, have "an excess of consciousness."

Certainly, an overwhelm of input is a core schizophrenic symptom, referred to as "ambivalence" and defined as the simultaneous experience of opposing emotions or rapid shifts between extremes of emotion, as well as unusual associations. Schizophrenics suffer from an inability to sort through the flood of options. A less extreme and more manageable flood of options can produce a mind with a gift for finding creative solutions to problems. I experience in a moderate way both states. Sometimes I can't make the simplest of decisions, especially in drugstores: which toothpaste? What brand of Vitamin C? But even with simpler questions such as, "Do you want to go to the movies?" I will be flooded with irrational possibilities, and confusion. Other times, a solution to a question arrives in the middle of the night, requiring just a little discipline to get up and write down the gem.

Author and biologist Rupert Sheldrake in *The Sense of Being Stared At* (2003) and *Dogs That Know When Their Owners Are Coming Home* (2011) took on the subject of psychism and creatures, including telepathy and precognition. Earlier, in his landmark book, *The Presence of the Past* (1988) he developed the term "morphic resonance" to describe the capacity of the greater mind of self-organizing systems to retain memory. Repeated patterns of events can be "inherited" from previous similar patterns, across spacetime, independent of material memory traces in the brain, or of information encoded by genes. This capacity, he postulates, is a kind of collective memory that enables evolution to proceed by way of "habits"—past successful actions that guide behavior and influence physical characteristics of the species. Even the so-called "laws" of nature, according to Sheldrake, are manifestations of morphic resonances. While I don't really understand how this might work, I appreciate his insistence that "mind" is not the same as brain and that minds of diverse beings interconnect. More recently (2017) Sheldrake has gone much further down this road, speculating about consciousness in the form of electromagnetic waves or thought waves with which our extended minds interact within the cosmos at large. The cosmos is conscious.

Sheldrake reminds me a bit of an earlier influence on my thinking. T. C. Lethbridge, an archaeologist and world explorer, delved deeply into dowsing—using the pendulum bob to map the psychic terrain. He believed that psychic messages are delivered in code, and that our brains translate them into our native language. In my account of animal telepathy in "Messages with Cats Attached," Bill the cat communicated telepathically to me in what I "heard" as English. Lethbridge explained how cat psychism could work, for example in their seeming to see through walls, through the vibrations detected by their whiskers; and that insects can detect their food through vibration including by way of their whisker-like instruments or bristles. Mind, Lethbridge believed, permeates everything, and "the pendulum seems to be confirming this." He also thought that ghosts are not conscious; rather they are projected pictures, similar to a TV image, except at a higher frequency. However, certain ghosts appear to have communicated with me, as well as with other people I know, contradicting this formulation.

While not agreeing with all his interesting opinions (and he was so modest, self-doubting, the first to say his schema could be wrong), I learned a great deal of what I know about pendulum use from reading him, and found his ideas quite confirming of my own experiences. The brain, he said, is just a censor, "suitable for earth-level thinking." *Mind* on the other hand could leap beyond sequential time to a level in which timeless information is stored. Using the precise counting of pendulum's swings and length of arc, he devised a system of measurement, and was able to correlate, for example, an insect's vibrations and the swing of the pendulum in relation to the insect's locating of a particular food plant. He speculated that a specific "ray" creates a path whereby an insect locates its own food source. He created a vocabulary with which to describe his ideas, using such as "bioelectronics," and "rates," (length of the pendulum cord), for instance though in other ways, terms he uses are out of date, such as when he refers to "five races" of humanity.

It seems as though everyone engaged with the transpersonal is struggling to help develop a vocabulary and research methods, descriptions, and specificities of the experiences. The term "transpersonal" itself, coined by Charles Tart, was used as a cipher for "spiritual." His small founding group of experimenters with parapsychology didn't dare use the term "spiritual" for their orientation, as he explained in a meeting at which I was present, because they would have been laughed out of the academy. Yet through their persistence they founded a field, combining their own techniques and experiences with those long developed in Asia (yoga, shamanism, meditation) and South America (ayahuasca and other herbal journeys), and have spread many of these practices into mainstream American and European education.

For four hundred years Enlightenment sciences have diligently fragmented our sensibilities, even as these sciences have expanded some of our capabilities as well as our lifespans. In bracketing the observers' emotions behind a wall of alleged objectivity, science has deliberately limited the possibilities of knowledge. This illusory objectivity is easily discredited, as feminist critiques have shown. Far more valuable is the technique of revealing one's subjectivity and motives for interest in a given field of exploration.

In contrast, poets generally court subjectivity and immerse themselves in emotions, even hoard them. Poets often use their skills to create a net of words intended to evoke emotions in readers and hearers. While scientists demand (have confiscated) "reason" as both the starting and endpoint of inquiry, poets often go beyond reason, using devices such as verbal music and rhythms, to provoke altered or exalted states.

Another self-imposed limitation of scientists is on what qualifies as a "source" of input. A poet can use the work of a scientist as a legitimate source, but science seldom feels confident to return the favor. In science publishing, mundane sources and personal experiences are often denied or hidden. Emotional motives or nonrational intuitions guiding research are seldom revealed. Anthropologists, like poets, experience altered states and witness paranormal phenomena in the field but mostly deny or hide these, perhaps sharing such experiences only with trusted colleagues in late night pub discussions, and not in published articles. They do this out of fear of losing credibility and jobs. What is the credibility they will lose? They will lose the safe label "sane," a category intended to separate out certain disparaged, even demonized, methods of knowing. While this is changing somewhat, lucky for me poets have always been able to be poets even if considered "crazy."

Social bias deeply affects what paths scientists are allowed to explore and what truths they are allowed to bring to public awareness. For decades biologists did not disclose observations about same-gender bonding in creatures, for instance. Social bias effects all of us, nevertheless it is shocking to learn, from Bruce Bagemihl's *Biological Exuberance* (2000), how much material on transgender, multigender, and homosexual bonding biologists have acquired about creatures and have left unpublished. We are surrounded by androgynous and sex-changing beings, and by homosexual pairs, and families centered on bonded females, as well as father-only parenting. Yet the fear of being discredited has sustained privileged mythologies such as creation as an exclusively heterosexual enterprise, not far removed from the ancient poets' imaginative and limited narrative of animals rescued from a great flood by climbing into a boat in heterosexual pairs, "two by two," which would leave a large number of species behind. These images continue to prevail even in a field as self-consciously "objective" as biology.

While purely materialist scientists deny experiences of psychism, or what could loosely be called "spirit," and attempt to exorcise any spiritual or poetic sensibility from accounts of the world, some of the most influential scientists and philosophers of science have also been artists or spiritual practitioners or both. The sixteenth century philosopher Francis Bacon, one of the founders of scientific method, was also a poet and included poetry among the three types of knowledge available to humans. In the eighteenth century, poet and novelist Johann Wolfgang von Goethe made important discoveries in anatomy, optics and morphology, the latter influencing Charles Darwin. The physicist Albert Einstein believed in the pantheistic, immanent god, a god who permeates everything, of Baruch Spinoza, and openly acknowledged the spiritual awe that derives from the study of science. He wrote:

> Everyone who is seriously involved in the pursuit of science becomes convinced
> that a spirit is manifest in the laws of the Universe—a spirit vastly superior to

that of man, and one in the face of which we with our modest powers must feel humble.

The contemporary biologist Lynn Margulis worked with her poet son in order to better detail the incredible life of microbes in *What Is Life?* (2000) and other books.

What all this means is that the "poetic license" available to poets is transdisciplinary and eclectic. Poetic license—to expand its definition—gives the artist carte blanche to be eclectic in sources, to bend language and image, to use singular occurrences as sources, to cross disciplines with the laissez faire of a cat on the hunt. The Greek and Latin roots of the word *metaphor* mean to "transfer" or "carry across" from one source to another. The concentrated use of a poet's mind and skill can be a valuable contribution to knowledge and understanding of consciousness. This is my hope with this book.

I came to a desire to see my stories of creatures reaching across as illustrative of specific transpersonal or paranormal occurences: synchronicity, precognition, psychic communication, and empathic encounters. I also began to categorize the nonbodied presences, visions, wraiths, and other experiences of more-than-human interconnection with feelings, thoughts, and intelligence, opening the possibility of a dialogue with some greater mind.

Panpsychism is a term used by those who have posited that consciousness pervades everything, that we are minds within a universe of mind. Philosophers who have held this idea include Plato, Spinoza, and William James; philosophical systems incorporating panpsychism include Greek Stoicism, Taoism, Vedanta and Mahayana Buddhism. This orientation surely also applies to many of the world's indigenous philosophies. The writer Paula Gunn Allen described this idea with regard to the creatrix "Thought Woman," of traditional Pueblo peoples in the American Southwest: "as she thinks, we are." Thought comes first, material reality follows. Animism describes peoples who relate to earth and all beings as sentient and feeling. They communicate their sense of relationship through ritual offerings, a gestural language of reach-across that weaves deep relationships with our co-beings on earth including natural forces, lakes, mountains, groves of trees. And for practitioners of ancient polytheistic religions, such as Yoruba chief and priestess Luisah Teish, ancestors are spirits of the departed who continue to be available and can be persuaded, through offerings and prayers, to give assistance to those who call on them. As I witnessed and felt on my 1997–1998 visits in rural South India, this sensibility continues, so that a deity (a village goddess usually) can take the form of a creature at any given moment and deliver a message.

Despite the encroachments of development and materialist-based education, the human world surely needs to reweave (continuously) its dependence upon and responsibilities toward the well-being of nature. As Lethbridge wrote optimistically in his 1976 book, published posthumously: "We are just at the start of what appears to be a science embracing all sciences." This needs to include the ecological sciences of indigenous peoples.

If humans and creatures really do share a psychic mind, there is little that differentiates us. This resonates with my own idea (Grahn, 1993) that human evolution took a turn toward ritual at some historic point millions of years ago, setting us on paths toward increasing amounts of cultural accumulation. This path includes, most recently, crafted and mass-produced objects (now strangling oceans and air). But that aside, except for the earlier and continuing turn to ritual (which I call Metaformic Consciousness) to now, we are not different from other creatures. Even the smallest and least "brainy" therefore must have consciousness, perhaps to a greater extent than we in mass culture do. We living beings share, in other words, a common mind or minds, which needs to be mapped so that we can further comprehend ourselves and the world.

The question is how to show the connections as demonstrably true and not our imaginings, our internal neurological storytelling. For this reason, in my pieces describing extraordinary reach-across between creatures, I have mostly selected examples that were witnessed by at least one other person. I am well aware of how one's brain can be a trickster, and how it wants to tell a story about what it perceives.

The experimental methods of science, though narrow in focus, can be enlisted to affirm certain transpersonal repeatable psychic skills. The physicist Edwin May and several others have established strong evidence, using scientific methods, that psychism is a real phenomenon, repeatable, and testable. May believes that nearly anyone potentially can have at least some psychic capacity, using an as yet unidentified internal sense, and that many people already experience this. However, he selects his remote-viewing test subjects from a small pool of extraordinarily gifted people who are seemingly able to turn on their psi capacities at will, even in a laboratory setting. To run his tests, he has stocked up three hundred photographs of geographic and urban sites with distinguishing features, such as a mountain, a smokestack and railroad tracks, three trees and a lake, a compound of buildings with a tower, and so on. In a closed room and under his supervision, his viewers go into a light meditative state and draw pictures of what they "see" in their minds. May uses random computer generation to select the target photograph, so at the time of the experience, the gold standard of science is invoked—double-blind conditions. In some of his later tests, the computer selected the target photograph *after* the viewer drew the picture, adding assessment of precognition to the psi experiment. He consistently obtained statistically significant results, that is, results not explainable by chance.

My own experience includes only a few occasions of precognition, mostly involving dreams, in which I see a distinct scene, and then the next day reality produces exactly what the dream portrayed. When I asked May how in the physical world this could be, he replied, "time bends," referring to Einstein's model of the spacetime continuum as a kind of net that is weighed down by gravitational objects such as our earth, enabling people (and therefore creatures) with an internal psi capacity to see ahead. Interesting that May says that while psychedelic and other mind-altering drugs may lead to a subjective sense of ecstatic awe, in actual discernible psi capacity, the drugs interfere.

May and other scientists are currently accepting the idea that consciousness is present whenever there is "processing of information." This description originates, apparently, with David Chalmers, who speculates about thermostats having consciousness, yet struggles with the "hard question" of subjectivity; a question that for me is solved whenever I include the heart area and other sources of our feelings (our glands, our microbes) as part of mind, being interactive, reflective, experiential, and may I add perhaps the most crucial, relational.

Another scientist who has been inspirational in her descriptions of life on earth approaches consciousness in relation to the activities within the cell walls of organic life forms. The microbiologist Lynn Margulis previously worked with James Lovelock on the Gaia theory of Earth as a living organism. No part of this earth is "uninhabited"; life abounds even in ice, in boiling vents at the bottom of the ocean, in the clouds, even in deep anaerobic mud. Joining forces with her son Dorion Sagan, a poet, they urge us "really to listen" to life forms in their elegant book on microbes, *What Is Life?*.

On a macro level, dark matter and dark energy are thought to make up 95 percent of the cosmos. Jamie Farnes, an astrophysicist at the University of Oxford, has postulated that the two forces are combined into what he calls "dark fluid," a substance that has negative gravitational polarity, and cannot be seen, as it does not reflect nor absorb, light. It constitutes a "sea" in which material objects, galaxies, comets and stars float. Galaxies, he speculates, are held in place by the negative fluid pushing against them, perhaps a "halo" of it forming around each galactic body, pressing it in place. He describes negative gravity as a force that, when you push against it, comes toward you. Once again, the image is of "ocean" with rivers and currents; perhaps, I'm thinking, a specificity, holding us, aware of us. I'm thinking of how secure I feel every time I experience life as a beloved community sharing common minds with other beings.

ONE

Three Accounts:
A Psychic Net Between Us

Three nonfiction pieces convey the idea that we inhabit an interconnected world communicating thoughts and feelings, even across very different species. Creatures at times feel empathy for us, just as we feel it for them.

Dragonfly Dances

As a child without television, phone, or any electronic distractions, relishing complete freedom during the long summer days when my parents were at work, I asked questions of wildlife. I lay on the ground eye-to-eye with fighting beetles and clashing pairs of praying mantises. I knew where the black widow spiders, the horned toads, and the crawdads all lived. I brought fearsome red fire ants home in a jar of sand to watch them replicate their home tunnels, to gape at their amazing labor of moving and hauling, building and cooperating. I watched them clean out their house and carry their dead above ground. I also knew how dangerous they could be; a toddler had to be hospitalized after getting trapped on one of their big sprawling mounds in a lot near our home. I had dropped my Levis to the ground more than once, shrieking with the pain of a red ant stinging my knee. But living close to them as they were safely encased in the glass jar, I was learning to love them as well.

Asking questions is how I came to closely watch Mollie, the wild cat in our neighborhood, in her hunt for the grasshoppers and mice that fed her. I saw how she swallowed a mouse until only the tail dripped down her chin and then watched it slowly slither into her slender inexorable maw. My nine-year-old self laughed until my sides hurt over this sight of the tail dripping out of her mouth.

As I trailed around behind wild Mollie, wanting to know her habits, I also wanted her to reach out to me in some personal way. She never did this, though she did give presents to a neighbor dog. A medium-sized young collie had been tied to a wire clothesline by neighbors who owned him. He could run up and down the yard, his leash sliding along the line as he barked angrily at everything that came into his view. Not much did, on those long hot nearly silent days. The first indication I had that animals reason and have compassion came from watching how the little gray cat lurked around the building near the confined collie, with a dead mouse in her mouth. She would wait until the dog was at the other end of the big yard, and then would trot over to drop one of her extra catches under the clothesline so the dog could reach it. While I thought this might have been coincidence the first time, I saw Mollie do this several times, and saw also that the dog found each little body and joyfully played with it for the better part of his otherwise monotonous days.

The little wild cat had reached across to the dog, with every appearance of empathy and decisionmaking. Perhaps this was the germinal moment of my desire to experience creatures reaching across species lines, and of longing for them to communicate with me, not pet to owner, but creature to creature. I wanted to know them, and didn't know how to initiate the dialogue. Would any of them reach across to me? Could I learn to reach across to them? The insects especially seemed challenging, as I didn't even know how to meet their eyes.

One day in 1995 my childhood desire to have a personal interaction with an insect—this time a dragonfly—was fulfilled. An encounter with a dragonfly is an encounter with a gatekeeper of spirit, according to the teaching of some indigenous people of the North American continent. The connection, usually initiated by the creature, indicates a major change in one's consciousness and therefore one's life.

My very personal dragonfly encounter took place summer of 1995, and lasted over an hour. My spouse Kris and I were playing golf with our friend Ruth, on the Willow Park course in Castro Valley. Ruth's ball had gone into the creek that runs the length of the course, keeping the place both challenging and life-filled. From TV images golf courses seem like human-only territory, but the municipal courses my friends and I play in the Bay Area are full of wild creatures. A blue heron lives along Willow Creek, as do hawks and snakes, rabbits and foxes, turkeys and coyotes; once, we saw a mountain lion on a nearby hill. So when I went over to help Ruth look for her ball I wasn't surprised to see something moving in the thick scum of algae growth covering the water at this particular spot. An insect about three inches long was persistently, if weakly, moving. Ruth came running with her long-handled aluminum ball retriever, and she got the cup under what we now recognized as a dragonfly. The rescue immediately looked like a cruel exercise in futility as we saw that the body of the creature was completely enmeshed in webs of slime, a mossy growth of algae in long thin intersecting lines that made a net-like cocoon around the struggling body. The largest dragonfly I had ever seen now lay helpless in the palm of my hand. Gingerly, I began to strip off the binding strands of slime. There were dozens of them. Would the dragonfly let me help? My fingers looked huge compared to the vulnerable, exhausted body in my hand.

We still had a golf game to play, and golf etiquette requires keeping up the pace, so we treated the creature as we walked along, at first taking turns holding it while we hit our shots. The creek area where we had found the dragonfly was the fourth hole, less than half way through our game, which is about a mile and a half in length. By the fifth hole she—I call her "she" because she was so large, and often among flying creatures the larger ones are female—was riding on Kris's shoulder, clinging with well-developed hooked ankles and feet to the cotton cloth of her T-shirt. Because my fingers are small I was best qualified to softly, softly unfurl the stubborn shroud of muck from the fragile body. Holding my breath I peeled layer after layer until I could see the structures of form, a long brown body, large dark eyes, two pairs of magnificent, delicately netted wings, now crumpled and stiff.

After I had stripped away most of the filaments binding her legs and the first of several layers of fiber from her wings, the still-encumbered creature made an attempt to fly. The flight consisted of a yard-long head-over-heels somersault to the ground, testifying to the fact that the second layer of muck, which had dried by now on the wings, was weighting them down and had caused their usually transparent fabric to crinkle into what amounted to an aerodynamic crisis. The dragonfly raised not the slightest protest when Kris picked up her upside down body and placed her again on her own broadly human left shoulder.

I went back to my restoration work, aware that drastic measures were indicated to solve for the crinkled, disabled wings. I pulled another binding or two from the body, and tenderly worked a few more strands from under the wings, of which she had two pairs. The coating on top of the usually transparent wings had now completely dried and looked to be a permanent cement, rippling their thin surfaces like bent airplane-propellers.

I set aside my fears that I would tear the fragile, brilliant instruments of flight and remembered the bottle of water always tucked into the pocket of my golf bag, along with extra balls, an old glove and a bag of raisins that had petrified in the heat. In a hurry, I raised the water bottle over the wing, aware of watchful dragonfly eyes. The sight of the bottle's metal form looming overhead immediately set off a creature alarm and her second attempt to fly. Again, flight was a breathtaking failure as the dragonfly catapulted head-over-transom onto the dry California earth. Again, Kris leaned down and picked her up, and again, the shoulder was solace and hope, as hooked feet dug in.

Now I became cognizant of a strong current of awareness beaming toward my eyes, and emanating from what looked like a little square organ on the dragonfly's head. I became certain that she was in touch with me, was thinking, and not only thinking, contacting me somehow with her thinking.

Smarter now and more patient, I wet my fingers first then slid them ever so lightly over the wings, first the two on the left, the most encrusted. The water dissolved the stiffened filaments, and allowed me to roll them. Now she was far from being in a state of panic; the dragonfly was acting as though she knew exactly what I was doing to help, as I could tell from her body language. She seemed to be making very conscious motions, turning and lifting her wings one by one, separating the upper and lower pairs so as to allow the needed access for my wet fingers, and enhancing the process of my tender work. Could this be true?

Giving up the golf game, I stayed completely in the moment as I rolled and rolled until the slime fell off each wing, which as it did immediately straightened. Elation! And—our conscious connection was not my imagination—the dragonfly *was* turning to engage my wet fingers, was guiding me into the next step and the next, turning to present her other side, and the undersides as well as the tops of each of her four wings, and also the last few filaments on her wire-like legs. We were working together! Delicacy of timing in joint effort did not fail us, and by the end of the sixth hole, the slime was off. One wing remained a little wrinkled, but the game of recovery was won, and this was clear to all of us. We relaxed. She would live.

With her long body as brown as the recently released mud, the dragonfly stayed still on Kris's shoulder. "Resting," I heard clearly as I stared at the head box between her large eyes, that appeared to emanate toward my mind, and now emitted a golden glow that opened my heart as well, a distinctive sensation that I experienced physically as well as emotionally. The insect foot-clutch on cotton cloth was confident, even as Kris hit her shots off the tee and fairway. When the golfer's left shoulder dipped, the dragonfly dipped with it, as though on a slender bough in the wind.

On the seventh hole, I noticed the change. It began as an underglow in various sections of her body, so at first I wondered if it had been there all along and I simply hadn't noticed. Then the blue color became more evident, then startling, deep and luminous as summer sky.

"Look," I said breathlessly to my companions, "She's a *blue* dragonfly." Here I should say that long afterward, doing a bit of research, I learned this was probably a male dragonfly.

The blue was that sparkling clean lake-water shade beloved of race car drivers and motorcyclists, and it spread until the whole body had it, except for the dark eyes and the darker box, that intriguing communicating shape that I could feel as well as see between his eyes, on top of his head. Then, amidst the blue, dazzling gold appeared as well, as though a whimsical, good-humored and patient painter had put golden trim on a particularly treasured model. We were all in love by then. Ruth and I continued to exclaim our pleasure and Kris glowed as she craned her neck to check on the condition of the creature who rode her as though she were the stablest of horses across this winding course. We were together in that state of knowing life had given us a beautiful and unexpected present.

Each hole on a golf course takes about fifteen minutes to play, so we had been with him for almost an hour. As we left the seventh hole the dragonfly turned his body around into the late afternoon wind and we sensed another change. "She's getting ready to leave," Kris predicted. I tried to keep my attention riveted so I wouldn't miss the take off, but as we walked up onto the eighth tee box, my sight wandered and didn't see till Kris called out. The blue dragonfly had launched and was already high above Ruth. Stopping still about thirty feet in the air, he performed a steep downward spiral dance, directly over Ruth's head, before twirling left and disappearing into the upper branches of the nearest tree.

My rational mind, always clicking away in its sometimes cynical fashion, said into my ear: "probably a practice spiral, not necessarily a dance of gratitude and fare-thee-well." But none of us believed that, especially because we were left in a happy state that lasted days afterwards, as happens from a visit with persons one loves intensely.

Rational mind is frequently wrong about these fine interactional moments, so I was surprised but not skeptical at our next encounter, which took place about a month later. That much time had passed before the three of us again played golf on the Willow Park course. As we approached the fourth hole, we were recalling that this was the place where we found the creature who had spent such a long time in our care. Deliberately I had worn the same hat and shirt I had on then, and my companions had on similar clothing.

The air directly above the tee box was swarming with dragonflies as we arrived, at least fifty of them, most of their bodies in the brown state, though a few of the larger ones were blue. Had they been gathering there for days? Were they gathered there on this day because of some food source or because every year at that time they gathered there? Or—as our lifting hearts told us—were they gathered there because we had been recognized and they wanted to perform a group acknowledgment? A dance for us. One, a particularly large blue one, came very near and looked into my face—and I could sense a connection. Once again, I felt the heart emanation from the head area, straight toward my own opening heart. He hung in the air about five feet in front of me, looking directly at my face. He flew higher and did a little downward spiral dance, twice. The encounter took only about a quarter of a minute but was very intense. After he left I felt a burning sensation in the lower left quadrant of my face, spreading to my heart, flooding me with goodwill. I have come to recognize this from my travels in India as a *shaktipat*, a sensual experience of eros, heart-opening spiritual love with extreme joy given as a *darshan*, a blessing. It is both physical and emotional, and I am unable to conjure it from my imagination, or from inside myself, alone. The sensation of intense heart-open love following this, evidently my second encounter with the dancing dragonfly, lasted about five minutes before fading.

But a mystery remained. My understanding of how the subtle energy jolt of heart-opening travels from one being to another, is through the gaze, the eyes emitting a potent charge of life-force. What, then, was this organ on the head of the dragonfly? A little research revealed this: dragonflies have two enormous compound eyes, one on each side of their faces, like domed windows with multiple—tens of thousands—of facets. But they have even more eyes. On top of their heads they have a triangular organ, the "occipital triangle," containing additional eyes, three small ones, called ocelli. The ocelli are more sensitive to light than compound eyes; they are connected to the largest nerve, and sensitive to UV light.

So this information on ocelli makes things more clear: I was seeing the base of an organ shaped like an isosceles triangle, my brain reading it as "box"; and within were three no doubt very shiny eyes, beaming loving energy in my direction.

Fortunate encounters with insects, moments of wonder, of rescue and recognition, of communication and camaraderie, of intense love and long memory, remind me that we are not alone here on earth, abandoned on a burning stone whirling mutely in space. We are connected in relationships of diversity, human with human, human with insects and plants, creatures and spirits, requiring only that we pay attention and stay still enough to think/feel the connection, and accept that we have been recognized, sent a vital communication, given a gift.

Messages with Cats Attached

The minds of animals have always interested me, as does telepathy among humans, which I have experienced more than a little bit. When animals communicate with me across the psychic plane I feel that a spirit of the universe is moving and I am riding in companionship with other beings. My stolid narrow sense of individual self falls away. For a moment something better replaces it, something connected and dancing, at home in the world beyond human interactions. I learned to trust this nearly indescribable feeling gradually, from a number of incidents, such as the following, which raises more questions than answers, questions of assumptions our culture makes about the substance and terms of reality, and the "real" or "para-real" nature of our relationships to the creatures in our lives.

Alice's Calling

One day in 1972 my friend Alice began talking about wanting a cat.

"Let's go get you one," I suggested.

"Noooo—the cat I want is a Russian Blue," she said, rolling a cigarette and looking up at me out of the corner of her eye, rather like a storybook Irish country woman, I thought. Though Alice actually grew up on the lower east side of Manhattan with nothing country about it.

I long admired this type of cat. Often I had gone to the glorious and of course sensational San Francisco cat show where I had never seen felines with so much fur or no fur whatsoever. The Russian Blues had gorgeous fur, thick and short, matching their intense bodies, supple with compact muscles, while their eerie silvery blue gray coats contrasted with sudden round green eyes.

"Besides." Alice was pouring a cup of coffee, taken black. "They are rare. Not that easy to find."

"Let's look in the paper anyhow," I insisted, pushing some of the junk off the kitchen table to hunt for a recent edition. At the time, we were living in the same house.

"No. I just want to think about it a while."

In the next few weeks we repeated this conversation at least three times. I couldn't understand her wall of resistance.

"Let's try the animal shelter," I would suggest. "The pet store."

"I just want to think about it, do a little meditating." In retrospect I recall that Alice loved to read about the minds of plants, and other ways the universe connects: it did make sense that she would go about acquiring a very particular cat through meditation alone. Alice's version of meditation, like mine, consists of lying flat in the bed staring out a window or counting ceiling tiles, while allowing random thoughts to flit around the hollow middle of her mind. At the time I didn't think of this as a very creative form, just a lazy habit we shared.

By March, some six weeks later, we opened the heavy oak front door for much of the day. The house was huge, three stories and five bedrooms, not counting ingenious uses of the attic and the back half of the living room. I already had two cats, Marmalade, a large red-yellow shorthair, and her white-furred, blue-eyed son T-Bear. Marmalade had a slew of boyfriends coming around that season though none dared come into the house.

What did enter the house one afternoon, with the sturdy swaggering motions of a little athlete, was a nicely muscled, shorthaired, densely blue-gray cat with round green eyes.

"Look, Alice," I exclaimed when she came home that night from work. "Here's your Russian Blue. Exactly as you wanted. He just walked right in the door."

She looked at him suspiciously.

"He's not the right one," she said.

"What? He's perfect—look at those eyes."

"He's not the one I had in mind," she said, and went upstairs to her room.

I was flabbergasted. Hadn't Alice called him to come to her? I couldn't believe anyone could be so picky. And I was certain she didn't mean it. Here was the rare Russian Blue, the answer to her description! And confirmation that she was correct, the world does have a psychic mind that responds to our deeply held desires. So I called the cat Charley and fed him, certain she would come to recognize him as what she had requested. He stayed.

Alice paid him no attention whatsoever, and as I hadn't intended to acquire a third animal, I didn't spend much time with him either. He didn't seem to mind our indifference, having his own agenda, and shortly after began an intense love affair with another household cat, T-Bear.

Marmalade's large son-cat was part Siamese. Though big-boned, snub-nosed and stiff-bodied like his clever mama, he was gentle and complacent; blue-eyed, he was completely white except for the tips of his ears, his nose and his tail's red rings. Slow and a bit strange, possibly a consequence of Marmalade dropping him down the ladder leading to the attic in one of her several family moves, before his eyes were opened. Once every two or three months he went up into the attic, climbed out on one of the outside eaves, posted himself precariously on a narrow external support beam to moan loudly for several hours. No persuasive tactics would get him down before he was ready. The rest of the time he stayed silent.

Though he was nearly two years old, I hadn't bothered to get him neutered because, following the Siamese hormonal path, his testicles hadn't yet descended into their sacks of fur.

T-Bear and Charley lay on the living room floor in each other's arms all spring, washing and chuckling, rolling and rubbing. On closer examination I noticed their sensuality had gone further. Charley frequently mounted the younger cat, gripping his white neck fur wetly to bump his stocky gray pelvis along T-Bear's raised backside. During their washing exercises, I could see thin pink penises protruding, revealing the eroticism of their play.

"They're lovers," I announced to Alice, thinking to rouse her from her indifference to Charley. "Isn't that fascinating? It puts a whole new light on tomcat fighting." And, I thought, here we are, all of us Gay, even the cats. But Alice put her morning coffee mug between her elbows on the cluttered table and wrinkled her nose.

"I want a sweet little Russian Blue. Female. That's all I'm thinking about in the way of cats."

Irritated by her ingratitude, recalcitrance, and blind faith in the power of positive thinking, I went back to observing the living-room lovers.

As spring stretched out, T-Bear began to fill out the round pouches of his testicular posterior, to smell a bit musty. His cheek fur puffed up thickly while muscle tissue gathered heavily on his bones as they outgrew his lean adolescence.

Charley changed too, though in behavior, not body. Where earlier he had been tender and sensuous he now became challenging and ferocious. He began hitting T-Bear and pushing him around.

He also began spraying his thick musk unpleasantly everywhere in the downstairs of the house.

Perhaps, I thought, if T-Bear were only a more highly developed being, he could have answered the challenge in kind, and Charley would have guided him into adulthood, and now in retrospect I believe that's exactly what Charley was doing.

Nothing could make a warrior of T-Bear. The male-ferocity friendship rivalry that Charley's behavior seemed to be trying to foster did not develop. Though T-Bear was much larger than Charley, he simply collapsed under the weight of the new expectations. I was horrified to find

T-Bear cowering for hours on end, having wedged himself under an over-stuffed armchair in the living room. In increasingly protective outrage I watched him avoid Charley, his ears back slinking from room to room on his belly, as if dominated by terror toward his lover-turned-bully.

The morning I came upon Charley pounding his round gray foot be-tween the red ears on the top of T-Bear's head until the white cat's chin audibly smacked up and down on the wooden floor, I decided Charley must go.

On the eve of this decision, Alice swept triumphantly through the front door with a slender gray cat in her arms.

"Here she is!" she cried. "I'm going to call her Freddie."

Incredulous, I went to look closely at the shorthaired, blue-gray, year-old female Russian Blue cat with the round, green eyes. "A woman down the block was holding her. When I told her that's just the cat I've been wanting, she gave her to me." Neither of the women seemed surprised to have found each other.

A one-woman cat devoted to Alice, Freddie was perfect, silky and sensual yet also full of mischief and fun. A housemate opened the re-frigerator one morning, shocked to find Freddie sitting in there, calmly, green eyes blinking at the light, having sneaked into the bottom shelf when someone was grabbing things out of it while gabbing to someone across the room.

Alice arranged for friends in the California countryside of Sonoma County to take tough boy Charley and get him fixed. The adults Freddie, Marmalade and T-Bear established an alliance in the house. Freddie was indeed sweet natured, and became Alice's close companion for at least a dozen years. Her confirmation had arrived: the world does have a psy-chic mind that responds to our deeply held desires.

And I continue to puzzle the fact that out of all the cats who could have walked through the door that season, only a Russian Blue did; why, out of all the women who could have been standing on the sidewalk on our block willing to give her cat away to the first person who asked for it, only the one with the Russian Blue female *was* standing there, in the moments when Alice, who spent most of her time indoors, was there too. What waves brought them all together to coalesce around Alice's desire? What wave sent the wrong cat first, and then accounted for him? Just exactly how do our minds, wills, and bodies interact with each other and with creatures across time and space?

The Nice Person of Bill

If it is true we can draw cats and other beings to us by putting our thoughts intensely into the biosphere, it is equally true that cats can influence us with the power of their own thoughts.

I learned this very clearly once in upstate New York, near Syracuse where I spent the summer of 1981 house-sitting for a friend of mine, the poet and writer Rachel Guido DeVries. Rachel had two animals living with her. One was an amiable hound-type dog, Scooter, while the other was an extremely willful black cat, Bill.

I call the cat willful because his method of getting into the house or any room in which I had enclosed myself for privacy was so forceful. He would claw and bang with his foot as though it were a fist, making explosions of noise slamming his body, as if willing to keep the din going for the duration of his life, though I don't know what his exact endurance was since I was never able to outwait his efforts. He quit the instant I opened the door for him, which I did increasingly quickly as the weeks of our companionship proceeded.

Middle of the night, he was particularly effective at making noise with the outside screen door, never finding it necessary to use his voice for the purpose of rousing me. The inside doors he rattled by shoving a curled paw underneath to jerk the door back and forth in its latch.

I explain this as prelude to the mystery of his behavior the first night I spent in the house. Knowing nothing of the cat's character, I read the general note of instructions Rachel had left on the dining room table, including the right percentage of canned food for Bill and Scooter. Being exhausted from traveling, I simply may have perfunctorily set some skimpy amount of food down for the two animals before going to bed.

The newly remodeled bedroom featured a gorgeous skylight directly over the pillow, through which I could see the stars of the northern summer sky as I drifted to sleep with no difficulty. In the many strange beds I sleep in, since my living entails so much traveling, I have grown accustomed to odd dreams and awakenings, even to other peoples' pets running up and down on me.

The particular dream I had that night was very odd, indeed I don't think it was a dream at all. For one thing, it had no pictures, just a firm, moderately loud masculine voice in my ear.

The voice said two sentences: "Bill is a nice person. Feed Bill."

Confused about where I was and who spoke so emphatically to me, I struggled to wake, then fell into slumber again. The firm voice came a second time, "Bill is a nice person. Feed Bill." This time I popped awake with genuine curiosity to find out where on earth I was. Who the heck was talking to me? I turned and saw the sliding doors on the sidewall, the outline of the bed lamp next to me. Already feeling an extra weight on my covers, I flicked on the light. Settled into the valley formed between my outstretched shins, and in that sphinx position characteristic of the species, there posed the cat of the house. His yellow eyes were fixed on mine with a penetrating stare that I began to understand had probably been going on for some time. I felt the wave of his will, which in the days to come I would come to know well.

"Oh," I said aloud. "You're Bill. What were you doing inside my head?" He got up, I got up, and we went to the kitchen where I fed him. It was 4:00 a.m.

This method of waking was never repeated. Either he didn't use his telepathy again or I didn't respond. Instead I put him outside at night and he switched to the door-banging game, which for all of its ruckus I found less disconcerting and easier to explain to other people than that his voice, in human English, had spoken inside my head.

Back in California seven years later, I moved into an apartment with a tuxedo cat, Percy, who communicated with me through telepathy, though I wasn't able to consciously capture anything as clear as Bill's lucid sentences that summer in New York State. One morning as I lay dozing, Percy settled on my chest with his chin lightly resting on mine. I startled awake, aware that I had been having a dialogue in my mind, in English sentences, and there were clearly two voices, one mine and the other a pleasant masculine one. Percy, I wondered? But had no way to check, nor could I recall the content of the discussion.

More obviously, Percy communicated by staring at me with great intention to communicate. This I am quite certain of, since I would often wake in the middle of the night to find him doing it. We had an agreement that since we lived in a second-floor apartment I would carry him down to the front door whenever he requested, even though his usual request could come deep in the night. Once or twice a week, if after his first attempt I fell into a doze, images of his face flooded my mind repeatedly until I opened my eyes and remembered I hadn't yet taken him downstairs.

Researchers have found that cats understand a vocabulary of about one hundred words, including such words as "dresser." Certainly a mass of pet owners testify that cat comprehension of human vocabulary includes their own names and elementals such as "dinnertime" and "want to go out." But *nice*? And *person*? Bill had a complex vocabulary indeed. How formal his syntax was, how reasoned his argument. Not *get up and feed me, I'm hungry*, but *Bill is a nice person. Feed Bill.* I was to feed him, not because he was hungry, but because he said, using the third person, he was nice. Does Rachel use the word nice a lot? I had to ask myself. Did Bill's choice of words stem from Rachel's approach? Or was the vocabulary formed in *my* head after the impetus of his will reached my brain waves? If this last scenario were the case, why would I not have constructed the sentence along the lines of *get up, feed the cat*?

The question of Bill's self-defined niceness and third-person personhood remain intriguing, including that the message only happened once. My pendulum, which I have come to trust for questions such as these, emphatically states that Bill constructed his own sentence, suggesting that nonhuman beings comprehend our language with greater complexity than what anyone has yet tested or verified.

Well, at least Bill was real. In my third example of cats in the psychic realm, the animal was like McCavity of T. S. Eliot's play *Cats*:

When you get to the stair. He isn't there.

A Spirit Cat

In 1982 I was only beginning to explore my own psychic capacities and had suspicions but no real sense of my life being full of spirits. By then I was living with a woman, the writer Paula Gunn Allen whose life is full of spirits, and began to recognize a few myself. It would be a long time before I realized that I grew up in a house full of them.

Ghosts and ghost stories have never much interested me, though I have seen reproductions of photographs claiming to be ghosts captured on film. A couple of times in my life the recently dead have stopped to deliver a message or two on their way to —wherever—but on the whole ghosts are not a part of my everyday conversation.

I was a little surprised and delighted then to detect a spirit cat in a house Paula and I had rented in El Cerrito, California. One early morning, we stood on the small wooden back porch while she smoked, the two of us talking vigorously but not directively, our conversations more like free association in a broad field of attention, with all kinds of creative connections surfacing unexpectedly between us. Suddenly I became aware that, even as I participated, I was also watching a small light-colored female cat who came up the porch steps, flitting past our legs and disappearing on the other side of Paula, nearest the open back doorway.

The cat just went into the house. This I thought as a matter of fact.

Abruptly I shook myself back into three-dimensional material reality, feeling like a character in a comic strip doing a double take. "Wait a minute. We don't have a cat." I peered into the house. No cat. "This is strange," I interrupted Paula. "I just saw a cat go into the house."

"Oh, I saw her too," Paula confirmed, describing at my request. "A small, gray cat. She just went in the back door. She ran past our legs."

We laughed about this mutual sighting; I always feel exhilarated by any sort of event on another plane. I wouldn't have thought much more about this incident than that we two were playing in each other's psychic minds, since while for us there obviously was a spirit cat, there were no other humans around to compare notes on the subject. I say we "saw" the cat—but realized it wasn't "real" immediately. This kind of seeing isn't exactly out of the corner of the eye. We turned to look directly at the cat. But it's a little like seeing something in a mirror. Everything is there yet something is missing, and you can't say what exactly: a missing dimension? How real flesh (and fur) reflects light? Somehow we knew this was a ghost cat.

"Probably that cat used to live here before it died," Paula speculated, our conversation turning to parameters of time and space for a minute or two before we went back inside and on with the day.

Later that afternoon we had a visitor from the East Coast. Excitedly we told her about our sighting, watching in disappointment as she closed her face in what could only be obvious disbelief. A woman directive in her attention, she was the kind to focus on real life and its problems and dilemmas with great success. So we dropped the subject and I didn't think about it again. How quickly any subject is stifled when it has no social matrix to give it confirmation and "reality."

Until early in the evening. After our first visitor left, we had a second, from southern California, our friend and fellow poet Eloise Klein Healy who also likes to engage in free-flowing associations in a broad field of mind. Nongeometric, we might say. Having worn out the slight bit of fun to be taken from jarring skeptical minds with tales from the psychic realm, neither Paula nor I brought up our morning's encounter with the nonmaterial cat.

After a brief tour of our living quarters and some admiration of the big yard and Meyer lemon tree, Eloise, sitting on the arm of the couch in the living room, looked up with a beatific, whimsical smile and said guilelessly, "Did you know you have a cat in here?"

"What's that?"

"I keep seeing a cat here in your house," Eloise said.

"Well, yes," we exclaimed.

On closer questioning, she described the spirit as a small, female, light-colored cat. We discussed what it might be. Someone who used to live in the house, we guessed, and came back to reminisce. Maybe run over in the street out front, I improvised, the idea lingering for some reason. What reason? "It is the house that matters," one of us said; "the cat pays no attention to any of us." So was it a ghost with a past and intention? Or was it an afterimage? A sort of movie-shell shadow sent from a different location altogether? An organic magnetic field caught in a loop? A forethought not yet born as a cat? At any rate, it leaped across dimensions to us and only on this one day. Had time bent that day and put us all as one mind into a different place? Or were we in a peculiar zone in which a spark reached out to connect all of us for one moment, a moment none of us ever forgot?

Science has begun to formulate experiments with results that support experiences of anomalous precognition, and the reality of psychic capacity. But so far no experiments show the possibility that through thought alone we influence the course of material reality. Or that cats speak from mind to mind and can convey precise English.

My friend Alice showed me that nature is responsive. You get what you request with your intent, spirituality people say, don't be swayed by the skeptics. Be a little patient. Just be sure to include *all* the important details, as you lie abed, meditating. Then wait: wait for the unpredictable, yet anticipated moment.

We are not alone on this planet unless we shut ourselves away from its myriad interactions. Whatever the reasons, these occasions feed my sense of profound delight at the interconnectedness of life: we are not just random dust motes blowing around, when, anyway, maybe dust motes aren't so disconnected either.

Interventions and Invocations

Consciousness has been defined as "awareness of self and others," increasingly acknowledged even by western scientists as present in all creatures, birds, insects, and fish. We reach out to them, try to know them; and often they do the same. How can we catch these incidents and take seriously that not only our companion animals, but wild creatures are responsive to us, and reach across at times? Methods have helped me shake loose from the pervasive and cynical box of mechanistic thinking. One way is to describe various communications out loud and establish them as real events. Another helpful method for remembering accurately, is to write notes down of interventions from creatures that seem aimed at solving problems, incidents that seem beyond coincidental.

The following set of true stories tries to differentiate among distinctly different forms of those incidents of conscious reaching—each of which involves "communication" of various sorts, some of it mysterious. The accounts begin with a straightforward reading by a human of another creature's body language and goes on from there into a cat's psychic reading of a human mind, and then into increasingly complex bending of spacetime.

Communication requires attention

Ruth had a perfect living situation in the bottom of the back of a house in the Oakland Hills. She used half her space as a workshop, and other half for a kitchen and sleeping area. Outside her front door stretched wilderness. Deer strolled past her door; her cats chased half-heartedly after ground squirrels and small rabbits; over the years she was there, large wild birds—hawk, owl—came to nest in nearby trees. With her quiet manner, the wildlife came close.

Ruth Rhoten was in the process of turning herself into a world-class metalsmith, able to raise a vessel from a single sheet of silver. She did restoration work for stores selling fine metal objects, but her real love was commissions for sacred objects—vessels for churches and temples, wands, rings, armbands, and once, a sacred knife for a Native American group in Northern California.

Her work area was thick with the tiny tools of her art, hammers, anvil, clamps, tiny punches and cauldrons, calipers, a delicate butane torch. Bowls and packages of semiprecious and precious stones—shards of blue lapis and carnelian, tiny rubies and emeralds—shared space with spools of wire and small sacks of priceless recyclable scrap metal, including gold and copper.

Her work table was set against the front window, so all day she sat on her work bench, looking up from the intense fine work to rest her eyes by gazing out the window at a meadow of a yard leading to a hill graced with tall trees—pines, eucalyptus, a red barked madrone tree. The closest neighbor once kept horses in a now-abandoned corral next door, so the sounds she heard all day were those of bird calls and the wind.

One day she was startled to see a deer, a full-grown doe, looking directly at her through the window, just feet away. When the doe did not move or change her gaze, after a few minutes Ruth went to the front door. The deer came closer, then veered to the north. Then returned. Then veered sharply north again.

"What is it?" Ruth asked. "What are you saying?"

The deer kept eye to eye with Ruth and repeated her motions.

"Do you want me to follow you?" Ruth took steps toward the deer, who responded by going further, then returning. Soon Ruth was trailing her across the long yard, step by step until they had reached the wooden slat fence of the neighbor's corral, long since vacant.

The doe leaped a low spot in the fence, turning to keep track of Ruth's eyes, so Ruth climbed the fence and jumped down. She followed the deer's shifting gaze to the door of a shed and pushed the door open. Inside were empty stalls where the horses once spent the night. Instead of horses, what she saw immediately was a frightened fawn; evidently the two had gone inside looking for leftover hay, and then the mother went back out but the fawn had gotten trapped inside when a spring closed the door, and the mother couldn't get it open again.

Ruth witnessed the happy reunion and watched as the pair trotted off into the wildness of the state park that bordered her yard. That was a straightforward interaction, the mother doe asked for assistance, and Ruth had presence of mind to take her seriously and affect a rescue of the fawn. However, Ruth had another interaction while she lived there that can best be explained as a mind-reading cat.

One of Ruth's clients had commissioned a piece that called for a metal collar around the stem, to be studded with tiny sculptures: the heads of four mice, facing the four directions, rendered in gold. Hard at work on the project, Ruth realized that she had forgotten what mice look like.

This problem was soon solved when Ruth found a newly dead mouse head carefully laid out on her work bench. Ruth was certain that her oldest cat, with whom she felt especially close, had brought the exact gift Ruth needed. She had never done anything like this. Amazed, the smith went back to the details of her work, and during the time she created the piece—using a process of lost wax—her evidently superbly psychic cat left an additional mouse head on her bench. And once the piece was finished, she never brought Ruth another mouse.

Speaking of mice, in my younger years I lived with a family of pet store mice, very clean and shiny, bright-eyed and healthy. I learned a couple of things about them by letting them have the run of my quarters and cutting holes in empty cigar boxes for them to build nests. I had never realized that they could gang up together and kill a larger creature, which they did one night to a hamster that had been sharing their habitat.

On another occasion I saw how "hands on" their mothering was, when a mother mouse made a nest in the bottom of my sleeping bag within view of my chair. One evening a young daughter mouse popped out of the nest to look at me. Her mother ran over, gripped her daughter's shoulders and literally shoved her back down into the nest.

The strangest event with a mouse: a cat had come into my yard and had been playing with a wild mouse for about half an hour, letting it run away, catching it, throwing it in the air. Sitting watching this, thinking of all the cruel stuff cats do with their prey to entertain themselves, I nevertheless refrained from intervening. Exhausted and dripping with cat saliva, the mouse sat still for a minute or two, and then leaped straight up and using one paw like a fist, popped the cat on its nose. Immediately the cat bit down and put an end to the fray; the cruelty was over. Leaving me with the distinct impression that the mouse had signaled, "enough," intervening in its own distress, and the cat had complied.

Insect Connections

Like many others of my mainstream US culture, which has through my lifetime divided creature life into "beautiful" and "ugly," and despite my best intentions, I can become irrationally frightened of many creatures, especially insects, in the past killing them wantonly and without cause. This mindlessness was brought to a crisis on my first trip to South India. There, moving into a rented house in an old venerable Brahmin neighborhood, the people venerated and protected life forms to a degree unheard of in the US mainstream culture, which teaches that insects (except those objectified as "beautiful") are, at best, "pests" and at worst disgusting and dangerous.

The house, lined with musty bookcases, and with no glass in the windows, harbored much life—mice, a wild cat, ants, large beetles, and two enormous spiders. In the first few days of living there, I mentally begged the lurking beetles not to fly across the room and land in my hair. But they did. When we ate at a nearby restaurant a mouse was racing around the perimeter of the room; I mentally asked it not to run across my bare feet, and it promptly did so. I asked it again, this time out loud, and it ran across my feet again. My fear grew, fueled by being among strangers in a remarkably enfolding culture I did not yet grasp.

My fear exploded onto the spiders—handsome, always together, strikingly marked in white and black, they lived high on the walls. When the landlord dropped by to visit, one of the spiders had gone into the kitchen; I decided "that was enough." I asked him to kill it, and obliging me, he did. Then began my grief as day after day I looked upon the survivor; I imagined his or her long life ahead, with no kin, no loved one, and felt the sorrow of irretrievable unnecessary loss. Perhaps sheer size—the spider was the size of my palm—allowed me to identify with it as a fellow being, with a life, with feelings, with kinships. Grieving in its behalf, I had to admit that my fear was not brought on by the large white spiders; I had projected onto them my fears of being in an unknown culture.

What else I have learned: animal psychics say that creatures don't comprehend the words "no" and "don't"—instead picking up on the other content of our thoughts and sentences. So, saying to the beetle, "don't fly into my hair" may have been interpreted as an invitation—through a psychic channel between us, one I hadn't realized existed. Anyhow, the landing in my hair scene was repeated three times, and that seems to me beyond coincidence.

Meetings with Remarkable Ants

Back home in the Bay Area of California, where I have lived for over forty years, I had a long acquaintance with grease ants, also called "thief ants;" they are tiny—between one and two millimeters (or one-sixteenth of an inch) in length. They send out solitary scouts who lay down pheromone smelling trails, and when they locate a large food source these trails gradually increase the good news until nearly the whole extended family arrives in neat columns. The colony that occasionally visited my apartment in San Francisco gave me a visual lesson about their selective taste in food on one occasion when I returned after being away for the weekend. On a counter in the kitchen, a long column of them was finishing the task of removing, from an open box of brown sugar, every speck of the brown. Brown sugar is white sugar coated with molasses, and this big ant family had meticulously carried away to their storerooms nearly every speck of the molasses, leaving me with a box of mostly white sugar. Very funny, ant humor clarifying that refined white sugar is not really a food group.

Years later, in a rented house in Oakland with a large kitchen, after I had accidentally left the lid off a jar of peanut butter, I found a colony of tiny ants happily carting the rich find away, in a busy column that was six members across, in two lanes, one line consisting of workers streaming to the counter, the other of workers going home with jaws full of peanut butter. At one-sixteenth of an inch apiece, each foot of the column contained at least a thousand of them, across eight feet of kitchen and another bunch of feet to the bathroom, turn right to the outside wall, out the window and down to the ground. Unknown numbers of additional feet or yards to their nest. A massive number of little beings coordinated in a complicated forage.

Wanting them to leave my kitchen, I intervened by removing the jar completely. Then I sat down to watch what I supposed would be mass chaos. I thought they would surely disperse at random, flooding my house with tens of thousands of them in their futile search for the precious jar.

"It's outside," I wanted to tell them. "It's in the side yard, near your point of entry." But I had no antennae, and no potent glands to emit molecules of smell that would convey meaning to them. We did not appear to have a psychic channel open between us. I soon saw that they were engaged in conveying meaning to each other. Amazingly, on the floor near the kitchen doorway they formed a massive star-shaped formation, a foot and a half across, with a dozen leaders in the center. Whose antennae were busy, busy, busy. Or maybe they took turns being leaders. They were having a meeting! My impression was that information was passed among one small group at a time, using touching antennae. There was also a lot of waving interactions going on within the lines leading to the central core of the star shape. After an hour and a half or so, a critical mass of them had gotten the message to return home, all leaving my kitchen along the column's orderly trail. No chaos. No mass frenzy. First have a meeting, receive new instructions, then everyone go home. Where, I would guess, scouts had already located the peanut butter jar in its new position outside. Success all around!

Ant Rescue Operations

One day sitting with a laptop computer on a coffee table I used as a desk, I accidentally set the machine on top of a grease ant, one of several scouts who were prowling around my room, drawn by some crumbs I had dropped on the floor while eating my lunch. Thinking the little being was dead, I moved my computer away and continued working. Fortunately, I had a magnifying glass within reach and was able to watch a remarkable scene. Three ants climbed up over the edge of my computer, bearing the injured ant. They stopped, and began manipulating her limbs and spine, which was bent at a severe angle, clearly broken. One after another each ran her own front legs, arms? Hands? Over the injured legs while the other two held their mate's body. They also attempted to straighten her spine, bent at the slender point of bridging her abdomen and her thorax. They repeated these very evident attempts at healing at least six times before giving up. Then, they carried the inert comrade off the computer, and hid the body under a newspaper that was also on my desk.

This was not the first time I had seen them intervene to resuscitate one of their own. Some years earlier when I lived in an apartment in San Francisco, a group of ants were busy dismantling an expired beetle in my bathroom. I noticed them doing what I thought was fighting with each other. The dismantling took several hours so I kept examining their actions, closer and closer, finally bringing a magnifying glass in to be sure of what I was looking at. Then I got it, they weren't fighting at all. Rather, some of the ants working on the beetle would fall over as though from exhaustion. Other ants would arrive through the opening in the wall and using their mouthpart—would give each of the fallen ones a drink, mouth to mouth. Experts on ants say the drink is a revitalizing liquid, a sweet syrup from carbohydrates, and feeding it to the fainting ones revives them to return to work.

Those are some of ant work habits, but one time I caught them at play, lounging on their own beach. In drought times I put water outside for the colony that sent members regularly into my house in Oakland. They were so much fun to watch that one summer when I had extra time to observe them, I placed a shallow, rimmed bowl of water on the floor of my kitchen and as soon as some ants congregated, lay down next to the bowl with a magnifying glass. The tiny, dark brown ants gathered around the wide rim dipping their faces to the water. They stayed in this area much longer than it took them to drink, which they did slowly, probing their mouths deep into the fluid. They socialized, moved around the rim, stayed still, gathered in groups of two, three, interacted with their antennae. In a sitting position resting on all four of their back legs, some ran their two front feet over their faces and along their antennae, washing up, or maybe a little self-massage. My impression was that they were relaxing in small groups as if they were people on a beach or at the bathhouse.

Every once in a while, say two or three times a week, a single ant would glide out onto the surface of the water. I could see that for their bodies the water was a thick consistency similar maybe to what jello or ice would be for our human bodies. The two occasions I witnessed the jello walk, the daredevil ant managed to return to the edge of the bowl and climb out. But as evident from the two or three bodies floating deep under the water in the center of the bowl, noticed every week when I changed the water, some rare individuals had ventured out, then had sunk in the dense liquid and drowned. Why would a few—very few—of the colony do this? Showing off? Young and adventurous? Practicing to become a scout? Do they act as individuals? The latest news from eco-biologists says yes, all groups of creatures include a range of personalities, some bold, some shy, some aggressive, some compassionate. Evolution cherishes variety and personality.

Insects talk to each other, but do they also attempt to talk to us? One day, I looked down at my arm to find a small brown ant vigorously touching its antennae to the fine hairs on the back of my wrist. I watched this one-sided interaction for a long time—minutes of my time, hours of ant time—and had a strong impression of witnessing someone trying to engage a conversation. Was this ant attempting to detect intelligent life on planet human? Having no way to consciously manipulate my arm hairs, I could not respond in any way, watching helplessly until the patient creature finally gave up. I can only wonder, and hope some clever naturalist devises antennae-like linguistic devices through which we can connect to these marvelous beings. We know insects as "workers," but do they also play? Do they communicate across species?

I wondered about cross-species communication one day watching a fly clearly seeming to play with my cat. She would land on his paw, looking straight at him, easily jumping up in the air when he tried to smack her. Again and again. Then she landed on his nose, jumping just out of reach of his open jaws, which he snapped together each time, lazily trying to trap her. They played this game twenty, thirty times. Was it my imagination that this entertained both of them? What motive did she have? Occasionally one of these very handsome medium sized houseflies, with prominent, curious red eyes and shiny green cape, explores the back of my hand, or stands casually on a finger washing its face. Why? Trying to figure out if I am suitable biting material? Or just keeping company? Science usually posits an "economy" of behavior, the continual practicality and utilitarianism of survival. But sometimes the interactions are unexplainable in those terms.

A Butterfly Talking
One morning I was in my garden in Oakland, sitting on the ground

planting young broccoli plants. Over the back fence flew two Monarch butterflies. I looked up, as they are always arrestingly gorgeous. To my surprise, they landed near where I sat on the ground with the seedlings. One butterfly stood directly in front of me, about two feet away, and interrupted my planting; the second landed a yard to my right.

The butterfly in front of me looked straight into my eyes with its bright dark eyes, and waved its antennae; as I watched, a monologue unfolded, and I sensed an urgency. I leaned closer; the butterfly moved closer too, never removing its intense gaze from mine. I moved my fingers in the dirt trying find a language in the rapid movements. I moved my head back and forth; I laid my cheek in the dirt. At one point, this butterfly flew over to the other, and they touched antennae several times, then it returned and resumed the one-way communication with me. Minutes passed; again, the near one went over to the other, and they touched antennae, then rose together in the air and left over the same spot in the back fence. I was astounded, and very sad. This attempted communication with me will puzzle me all my life. This beautiful creature took a long time to try to convey her or his message to me, trying mightily to tell me something, but I could not determine what it was.

Some people believe a butterfly can be the spirit of a dead person, though I did not have that understanding of this particular interaction. Butterfly antennae are sense organs, especially of smell, but also related to orientation; they are like radar. Later, thinking about it, I came to wonder if perhaps the butterfly approached me because I am a poet, and a poet in Mexico at that time was a leading voice in trying to protect monarch butterflies from loggers. Poets in India have also led fights against environmental destruction. Shortly before the two butterflies approached me, loggers in Mexico had burned a monarch habitat filled with the creatures, in order to stop environmentalists from protecting the region and preventing logging in the area. While I thought this— speculative as it seems—might have been the message, I did not have any idea what to do about it, besides mentioning the existential loss of habitat threat to monarchs at my public events.

This was one of the saddest episodes of my interactions with creatures—that a butterfly tried so hard to say something to me and I could not understand the meaning, I could not comprehend the language, a language of semaphore without flags. I felt trapped within my limited humanness, or incapacity to use my psychic functions at will.

My accounts of interventions so far have been mostly benevolent. A deer asks for help and receives it, a cat reads her caretaker's mind and does something helpful; ants hold a meeting, two of them try to heal a third one who is injured; and I had the privilege of observing. Sometimes though, an interaction with creatures has sinister overtones, and the intervention requires its own intercession, a conscious adjustment. So far, I've been describing interventions as living beings reaching out to make a positive adjustment or expression. Not a skyhook, that mechanistic metaphor of Daniel Dennett's, implying a cosmic all-knower reaching down, but rather a conscious reach *across* on the earthly plane. An invocation is different, often a calling in of a supernatural power, invoked because of a need for an intervention. In the next episode I am wondering if emotions, especially when they are the result of trauma, are such powerful connectors on the cosmically unconscious level that a kind of energy vortex can whirl into existence, catching up even the creatures and drawing them irresistibly into a destructive net of mysterious events. Can a human family's bad habits so impact the atmosphere around one of its members that a magnetic vortex draws creatures into it? This may have happened to me, with small birds.

Invocation of Birds: "I am an amending person"

The sparrows began throwing themselves at me soon after I had an idea for a story. I had already named it "Wounded Sparrows of Chicago," and made some notes. Based in truth about my early family life, the story would use a child's voice to link two kinds of dreadful episodes. One would be of my brother sexually molesting me in secret; I would link this to another of his habits, that of shooting birds and if they lived, bringing them home for my mother to feed until the poor creature was well enough to turn back into the wild. Though I was now in my fifties, I had not yet found ways to write about my early life, and this seemed promising—a way to suggest a connection between two forms of cruelty in our culture.

Two weeks later, I dreamed of looking into a room (as though with fish-eye lens and somewhat distorted perspective). On the floor was a brown sparrow. That's it—not a complex dream—image of a messy sort of room, a bedroom, with a wooden floor.

The next day while I was on the phone with my friend Jack, suddenly I sat upright and interrupted him. "I think my dream is coming true, have to go now."

Something had made a compelling noise and fluttered across the half open door.

Opening the door all the way to my bedroom, I saw my messy room that looked remarkably like the dream room, and standing on the wooden floor, a young brown sparrow. I saw he had drifted through the open window, on his way to learning to fly, and I could hear his family's anxious chirping in the eaves next door.

Urging my excited cat to exit the house and using a soft towel to pick up the sparrow youngster, I got him out the window into a safe return to his family. He was the first of ten birds to visit me in the next six months, as I worked on the difficult dramatic story of a family that injured and killed birds as a part of their emotional projections. A way they expressed themselves without using words, and without looking directly at what was happening between and among them.

It seemed as though every time I worked on the story another bird arrived. A sparrow crashed into the plate glass window six inches from my face as I drank coffee one morning in a sandwich shop, perhaps crippling herself; another lay dead at my feet as I walked into the post office a few days later. I recall hearing the voice of a worker inside that morning declaring in an outraged whine, "It is not in my job description to pick up some damned dead bird." But it did seem to be *my* job description. What was going on?

They weren't all sparrows. Playing golf one Saturday, my ball hit a young robin who died in my hands as I sobbed over her. They didn't all die: the two hummingbirds each rode my broom out the open back window as I lifted them toward freedom in an agony of patient silence, one centimeter at a time. "Just hang on," I said, "just one more second."

The jay fell down the chimney one rainy night and made his own way out, and about that time I had a second precognition dream, this time of a dead bird, and the next day another blue jay body lay in front of me on the path, and later that weekend a big woodpecker or some other medium-sized female threw herself at the tall glass window over my head for at least two hours while I was at school. I could think of nothing else nor turn my gaze for more than a few moments from her frenzy, and then went home to work more on my story.

Trying to understand why the birds were arriving, I took another look at the plot—was I writing it incorrectly? Were the birds trying to deliver a message? I had finished the story—I thought. But perhaps something—something that lives over on the other side of any singular consciousness—didn't agree. Thought I should keep going until I got it right. Was throwing birds at me until I got the message.

By July of that year I had another insight. I had been characterizing the air gun–shooting brother in the story as the only bird killer; but perhaps the little girl was also implicated. She would grow up, like me, and keep cats. An incident drove this point home shortly after I had begun noticing a pair of doves who nested in a tree across the street from my house. The dove pair, who were so lovely—soft charcoal and specked and so connected to each other, but one day my overly helpful cat brought me their fledgling, dropping the body at my feet. I realized that keeping a cat who lived outdoors was helping to destroy the birdlife on my block. That week I began to notice the deadly count: thirty cats lived on our block and only about ten beleaguered birds. I had lived there for decades, long enough to recall that earlier there were many more birds, but I had been unconscious about one of the primary reasons for their disappearance. Like the character of the brother in the story I had been unconscious about the harm I was doing.

So, I changed the story by adding a softening of my portrayal of the brother character, and also decided to write these notes in part to take full responsibility for my own part in the decimation of birds, especially through my love for keeping cats. Is love the be-all and end-all of life, especially of a responsible, spiritual life? No, I decided, not unless it is accompanied by consciousness, empathy for all beings, and courage to make change, including oneself. I love cats, my brother loved hunting. In the course of completing the story, my old, and beloved cat died; I decided never to keep another outdoor cat. Amazing how many years it took me to realize my own part in destruction of nature. Partly because I kept thinking of cats as "nature"—but they are not, keeping them as pets makes them extensions of human culture whether we acknowledge this or not.

After I changed my story and began these notes, by now several years following the first draft, another wild bird appeared in my life. This one was a pigeon with evidently some kind of wing injury, who showed up one morning in the little walled patio outside my front door. I put out water and food while it rested for a couple of days, and then was gone, recovered I suppose.

During this same period time someone interviewed me, on film, about the last half of my life. As I was recounting this story, that birds would mysteriously appear, a hummingbird suddenly bumped against the window six feet away from us. "Like that," I said.

Were the birds appearing to me as a message to stop writing the story and take full responsibility for the stress of their lives? I don't discount this possibility, given my sense that there are some kinds of "common mind" within nature, the explanation that makes most sense assuming that creatures and other life forms bring us messages or otherwise undertake interventions at times.

I decided to shelve the story for good.

I also asked Luisah Teish, a traditionally trained and initiated spiritual teacher from the West African and diaspora Yoruba tradition, what she thought might be happening. I explained to her how wild birds threw themselves at me in alarming ways each time I worked on the story "Wounded Sparrows," and told her the general plot. She replied thoughtfully to my question, saying that the story had so much emotional content that I was inadvertently "invoking the birds." She advised me to go outside and spread birdseed while telling the bird world that everything was okay, they did not need to come to me. She said, "Say this to them: 'I am an amending human, I am an amending human.'" So I did that. No birds throwing themselves at me in the years since then.

This story illustrates to me the existence of an interactive web of thought encompassing participants of life on earth.

The British science philosopher Rupert Sheldrake describes spacetime as having memory, which he calls 'morphic resonance.' Rather than imagining nature as having fixed "laws," he thinks that spacetime is a net of *habits* that guide evolution, structured as a fabric that imprints and adjusts, remembers and listens. The mind is not only infinitely larger than the brain in its calcium cage, each individual mind intersects with other minds across a spectrum of relational happenings.

In the story "Wounded Sparrows of Chicago," my family's long habit of injuring children is paired with its equally problematic habit of injuring, and then nursing, small birds. In a span of weeks of writing the story of myself as a child injured sexually by an older brother who also wounded birdlife—events that had happened fifty years earlier—I experienced birds crashing into my life, some injured or killed, some not. But all of them in some form of distress. I had worked hard on healing myself from the abuse of childhood; now I had to face that the bird world was not healed.

An idea of why: the "habits" that Sheldrake credits as the source of evolutionary propulsion, and which are housed in the atmosphere around us, inhabit his idea of "morphic resonance," or spacetime retaining memories of events. As a web of habit, in this case woven by perhaps centuries of my family's shooting of birds and then, inexplicably, nursing them back to health. In trying to disrupt this horrid sacrificial habit by writing about it, I had inadvertently perhaps triggered a vortex of chaotic energy that trapped the birds in my family's or just my own, extended energy pattern. With my highly charged emotion, I have created in this case a destructive vortex, a "spell" of sorts, that pulls individual birds into it through the power of magnetic emotion produced by my telling the story, writing it down, making it conscious. As though I pulled the cork out of a pressurized bottle. Now my task is to try to break up that pattern.

The solution involves communicating directly to local birds with a gift of seeds, and the spell-breaking sentence/thought "I am an amending human." I feel as though I am addressing the "collective unconscious" of neighborhood bird-dom when I do this practice; or addressing "the god of birds" if there is such a higher form in my world. Anyhow, I tell this true story because to me it so clearly reveals not only the obvious link between one kind of abuse and another; it also indicates that the world around us is conscious, relational, and interactive, not mechanistic. But not easily understood, either. Emotion is a major factor in common mind—the mind that both permeates and goes infinitely beyond the parameters of our skulls.

Kitty the Animal Rights Dog

In the 1980s two of the housemates who lived with my friend Alice broke with her "cats only" tradition and brought home a dog—a red wire-haired terrier mix with yellow eyes and a pleasant disposition. To calm Alice's anxiety over this being a dog and not a cat, they called her "Kitty." Almost every day Kitty went to work with Alice and Carol, who owned a coffee shop-bookstore combination that featured a small performance space. They worked long hours but Kitty did not mind, lying on the cool tile behind the coffee counter or saying hello to her favorite customers and letting them put ribbons on her collar and a red handkerchief around her neck, or best of all, taking her for long walks around the neighborhood. She was mellow and amiable, though with a terrier's avid curiosity.

Then one day Kitty stopped being diffuse in her attention and became exceedingly focused. Usually a terrier's attention rivets on such things as rabbit smell, or the sight of a furry tail disappearing down a hole in the earth. But instead of these sorts of hunting delights, Kitty's attention became fixed on Tina, the third member of their household. Tina spent most of her days at a job and went to the coffeehouse to help out only on weekends. Now, she took on a project, a commitment she made after attending a workshop on ethics and animals.

Tina had decided to do a presentation at the coffeeshop on animal rights, a project that required some heart-wrenching research. From the moment she decided this, Kitty hardly left her side. During the evening and on weekends Tina sat at the little desk in her room, reading and making notes. Kitty sat beside her. When she went downstairs to the household's bookshelves to hunt for a magazine or reference book, Kitty trotted along with her.

Tina knew that the material she wanted to present would upset people, that no one wanted to know how chickens were housed in the new factory farms that were replacing mom and pop rural enterprises.

On the day of the presentation, a Sunday, Tina was nervous; she wondered how people would react to her talk. She was not used to speaking in public, so she worried about how well she would do it. Kitty came too of course, making the rounds to say hello to people she knew. Then she went to the front of the store where Tina was setting up her chair and arranging papers and microphone. By the time she began to speak, Kitty was no longer sitting by Tina's side. The terrier was at the front of the stage area, her whole body in a rigidly alert posture, her gaze fixed in front of herself, on the audience. Everything about her said, "You pay attention now."

Tina made her way through her difficult material, about chickens having their beaks snipped off so they won't peck each other, as they are packed in such small quarters, of pigs kept in the tiniest of compartments all their lives to reduce costs, to be cost effective, to be competitive, and all the other justifications of our cruel food delivery systems. She talked for an hour and a half, during which time Kitty never wavered from her chosen post.

I know just how fixed Kitty's attention was, because, drawn by her behavior, I deliberately and to no avail tried to distract her. Tina, wrapped in her delivery, was unaware of the dog's unusual behavior though she would of course have been pleased at having such avid support. Was it support? Did Kitty know the content of Tina's talk and want us all to become aware (and do something about) animal treatment in the food industry? Tina's talk did not mention dogs or cats, she was discussing pigs, chickens and other traditional farm animals. Was Kitty operating from empathy? Or, did she sense Tina's deeply emotional upset, and was trying to comfort her? But in that case, why wasn't she at Tina's side onstage, instead of out in front of her in guard position, staring fixedly at the audience for an hour and a half, something she had never done before, or afterwards?

I don't know Kitty's motives for certain; I do know that if a human had acted as she did, "empathy" would have been the obvious explanation. So why not believe this of Kitty? Once in a while, a creature's gesture is so obvious, there is no doubt that it's a conscious reach-across of fellow creature sympathy.

Coyote Tears

The ranch should have been designated a nature preserve, it harbors so much wildlife. Oaks spread out in their usual generous pattern leaving lots of space for wild grasses and the carpets of fuzzy soft sage that fill the air with musky perfume every time it rains. Two kinds of owl, barn and screech, share space with a black night heron and numerous hawks and vultures. A bald eagle has been spotted more than once, while a family of large ravens has made a home, hunching their long shoulders like a parody of nineteenth century undertakers, standing high in trees lining the two-lane paved highway leading to the ranch dirt road. Dozens of types of flitty, talkative little birds, of lizards, salamanders, snakes of every description including rattlers, and insects beyond count, who fill the ranch air with their talking sounds.

Ring-tailed polecats, raccoons, skunks, and bobcats fill in the middle evolutionary niche, along with a family of seven or eight coyotes, who carelessly leave their scat everywhere, and howl as a group on occasion, their young ones joining in with yips. Despite this evidence of their presence, the coyotes keep to themselves and away from the humans, though rarely can be spotted up the road a ways, taking turns rolling in dust to suffocate their mites and fleas, while their leader, a three-legged old female, keeps watch. One year late in the rainy season, track was seen of a mountain lion, its paw print left in mud on the run, as wide across as the spread fingers of a woman's hand.

That woman was Sonia, who lived with her husband in a trailer on the ranch about half a mile from the main ranch house. She worked as a teacher in town, while he did heavy work on the ranch and they both kept the garden that fulfilled their dream of great fresh food. After a couple of years, they added chickens, then geese, and finally a small family of goats in a little corral near the house.

Sonia and Jim had seen the goats through their trauma after the mountain lion came through again, this time surmounting the high wooden fence into the corral. Deep in the darkness of night she leaped to the top rail and took aim. The billy goat ran frantically around, dodging the great tawny ball of muscle and claw to no avail, and his two wives and grown daughter watched the carnage as the lion patiently hauled the goat's long body over the fence and feasted on the remains for hours, leaving only just before dawn.

Sonia found them staring through the rails at the disheveled body of their lost relative, still shaking. She did her best to spend more time to comfort the survivors before driving to work in town, but within a month, one by one, each goat lay down and died. It could have been a portent, were they people who believed in such things.

Sonia especially grieved for her little flock through the short California winter. She had loved the whole procedure of milking them, and the challenge of getting the right equipment for making goat cheese. She had loved the horizontal dark bar of pupil in their startling amber eyes and the clack of their small hooves on hard-packed ground. She had loved rubbing her fingers along their long noses and pulling ever so gently at their ears that were soft as the furry sage in the meadows of the ranchland. This year she started her spring garden a bit late as with the goats gone, she needed to grow greens only for the chickens now. To cheer her, Jim arranged a trip to Mexico. "We'll go to San Carlos in Baja for the music festival," he promised, and so they did that, letting someone else tend the tiny farm they had carved out of the wild ranchland around their trailer, for the twenty days they would be gone.

A drunk driver on a narrow road changed everything; Jim returned to the trailer on the ranch after six weeks in a hospital recovering from severe concussion. Sonia was killed instantly in the head-on collision. Jim had come back just for a few days to say his goodbyes and pack up their things, giving hers away to people in town. He was going to live with his parents.

In the late afternoon on one of these days, the sorrowing man sat out on the trunk of a fallen oak tree, staring at nothing, just breathing the mountain air, thinking about his life here with Sonia. Then, a coyote stepped out of the brush and came within ten feet of him, sat down, and began to howl. For several minutes the animal wailed, before trotting back into the brush.

I've heard many stories of domestic dogs howling when a person they know has died. Given the depth of emotional commitment between humans and the creatures who live with us, those that we call "domesticated," the sharing of mutual grief at death of a member of the community is understandable. The coyote story, a true one, as are all the stories in this section, suggests we need to expand our idea of "domestic." Our home is wherever we live, and our relatives are the life forms who also live there.

Coming back to thinking about those birds throwing themselves in my life: if it is true that some kind of "valve" in our brains or bodies regulates the amount and kind of information or energy/bioelectricity that pours through us at any given moment, then couldn't it also be that the birds were pulled into a vortex around me by some kind of atmospheric valve collapsing that keeps them on their own life courses? Or is sending messages to humans part of animal heroism just as we send them messages and pull them out of forest fires and divert them from poison and nurse them back after oil spills? If we take extraordinary steps to aid and communicate with creatures we have no intention of then eating why wouldn't this work the other way too? And not only creatures who live in our houses with us, but also those we call "wild"? Life, after all, is about a great deal more than survival. Life is also about joy, love, curiosity, and endless interaction. Life is about heroism as well as self-preservation, and maternal feelings as well as rivalries. And life, perhaps, is also about interventions and invocations. Moments of reaching across to respond to an urgent feeling, and assist or otherwise touch, another being.

The Tender Touch of a Lizard

Peggy Lauer was a student of mine, in an MA program. She had been a career environmentalist activist, burnt out by the relentless detailed demands of years of endless meetings and other chores of fundraising. She realized she had become disaffected from her job, and at the same time disconnected from nature. She wanted to know how to reconnect.

I gave her the assignment of just sitting in some natural setting, in privacy; "do it every day for a set period of time, like an hour, and just see who shows up." I also told her to think about the term "merged identification," to try to find common ground with the beings around her. Peggy chose to sit under a coral tree deep in her Southern California backyard, and for a while nothing appeared to be happening. Then she began to notice a family of lizards who lived in the area. And they began to notice her:

On several occasions in my backyard, the lizards did not move as I sat or reclined near them, if I moved slowly enough. In the garden one day a large lizard came close to watch me. We eyed each other in sidelong glances for a while, and then without forethought I started to sing a lullaby that I sang to my infant son sixteen years ago. I sang the first four couplets of "Hush Little Baby," and suddenly the feelings I had nourishing my baby in my womb, and after his birth with my milk, rose up as I sang and looked at this lizard. Tears filled my eyes, and I felt a mix of joy, love, gratitude, and sadness. My heart completely opened, and it felt expansive and electric. I loved this lizard in front of me. As with the love I felt between my baby and me, I had generated a deep feeling of love with other beings in this connected world.

Peggy had made a connection to the lizard family through feelings of family, and of caring for another. These feelings then evidently were reciprocal, as evidenced by what happened later:

a young lizard came out from the bushes, crawled up a step, and put a webbed foot on my shoe when I sang "Hush Little Baby"—the only magical song so far in my repertoire—as I watched her. I looked to see if ants were close by, thinking that was what drew the lizard to my foot. No ants. When I looked at the lizard looking up at me, with that tiny foot still on mine, the loving energy in my body from the perceived sweetness of that touch burst through me into laughter, a fullness of feeling that I equate with love as connection, love as a falling away of separation and into a merging with another creature, an entrainment with the lizard and the wood of the step, the ground, the air, the warmth, the instant in the cycle of time that we shared. I felt it only for an instant. However, it had a deep effect on my expanded sense of self.

Sharing a Common Mind

These accounts display a lot about empathy and collaboration among creatures, toward each other, and toward human beings. Tender feelings, even cross-species, are not the province of humans alone. What is newer information, is that insects also experience a range of emotions, and sometimes reach across to us.

A second theme in these examples, is that of telepathic events, moments of stepping into a shared or common mind. This sometimes surfaces through dreams, or visions, or in other ways, as when the beetles landed in my hair. Rupert Sheldrake's idea of nature retaining memories of our behavior as "habits," or "morphic resonance," is one explanation for how, or more accurately, why, telepathy works.

The existence of paranormal knowing, or psi, has been validated in the research of physicist Edwin May. In his thirty-five years of studying parapsychological phenomena, May has been able to set up double and even triple blind tests using psychically skilled people with special skills in "remote viewing;" the subjects are able, with more than probable accuracy, to make drawings of scenes called "targets" located far away, and in some tests, randomly selected by computer software. How might some people be able to see across distances and into future time? When I asked May, he said, it is the nature of time itself that holds a possible answer. Space and time, as Einstein described, are interwoven as a fabric that bends in the influence of matter with its gravity. So a curved wall of future spacetime may be perceptible to some as yet not detected organ, a sixth sense, that we each have, though only some of us access.

And if humans have this, why not other creature life as well? Perhaps they have never shut themselves down, and therefore access much more of this common mind than we do, on occasion reading and acting on, our thoughts and feelings. Not only creatures who live as companions with us have displayed this, the mouse and beetle running across my foot did as well, and so did Ruth's gift-bringing cat. Other connective methods, portals of communication, in the examples I have described include precognition, dreams with messages, empathic behaviors, physical touch and gestures.

The wild birds crashing into my life as though caught in a historic madness, trapped in a "morphic resonance" of my feeling-driven invocation, seemed yanked into an energy vortex of my family drama which they continued to act out from the magnetism of my story, until I broke the spell. I know how strange this sounds, yet I have no better explanation. Inadvertently I was "invoking" some collective spirit of small birds.

All the stories imply that the creatures around us are full of family feeling; they protect themselves yes, and they are also capable of empathy, they try to help. On occasion, when we are open and invitational (even accidentally) they respond. I can change my own practices, tell my stories more consciously, try to steep them more in the wonder of life and less in the pathologies of human psychology. We can be amending persons.

TWO

Four Stories
Senses, Feelings, and Illusions

The four stories in this section convey ways we project and misinterpret, even hallucinate, the behaviors of fellow creatures, especially when we have only our five physical senses to guide us. The stories are creative nonfiction, in that the human characters have been disguised, or in the case of Clovis, are a combination of people. However the creature accounts that accompany the humans are all completely, literally, true from my own close observations and experiences.

A Hunter and His Horns

Ellen married Helmer for the boldness of his black moustache, a fine growth so broad that in his early twenties he waxed the ends and turned them rakishly upward whenever he felt optimistic. The pomade he used on these occasions combined beeswax and coconut oil, giving his face a scent that intrigued Ellen, and he could dance as well. She happily drove to dance halls and bar parties with him and said "Yes" the moment he mentioned marriage. Though neither of them had completed high school Ellen felt that with such passion as the moustache indicated, Helmer could catapult both of them to success.

Alas, after their first two children were born the passion indulged itself not in ambition but rather in drinking and gambling with like-minded companions in bars and alleys, leaving Ellen at home to raise two rambunctious and amazingly rude daughters. The siblings had both left home when she surprised Helmer with the announcement of a pending third baby, just when they had both believed their marital road might get easier. He adored this child, who resembled him except for being a girl, and proceeded to treat her with great attention, as though she was his heart's desire, a son. This exasperated Ellen, who attempted to counter the gender pitfalls every way she could, fearful that their last daughter, Janey, would not be wily and sharp-tongued enough to protect herself once she hit adolescence, and would not fit with her peers. Janey's peers, meanwhile, were kids who demanded toughness from each other.

Seeing Janey come home bruised or crying or cursing loudly from school week after week hurt both parents and made Helmer tug hard on his moustache for hours as he sat trying to solve the dilemma. He wasn't getting along with his boss at work in the steel mill either, and the combination of situations, his own and his daughter's, brought him to a conclusion. "We are moving to the southwest," he announced to Ellen as she stood ironing his thick trousers.

"What for?"

"My friend Everett has written that life near the border is much easier than here, weather's better, people are easygoing. It's the wild west, they don't care so much what you do." Secretly he was also thinking that no one would mind his whiskey breath so much as his supervisor at the factory did, and he would no longer be in danger of stumbling into some horrific piece of moving equipment or dropping dead from blast furnace heat or getting spattered with drops of fiery red metal from a leaky mold.

And, he could raise Janey any damn way he pleased. He could become a hunter, and she would come with him on trips. She would be a hunter too. He didn't say these things to Ellen, and without much more discussion, they packed up and moved.

"It's easy," his friend Everett had said, watching Helmer hand-roll a cigarette to near perfection, then light a kitchen match with his thumbnail. "Just tell them your craftsman background, and your history of supervision of other workers at the mill. How the management trusted you to do the measurements for quality control." Everett had just bought a four-bedroom house on an acre of land, working in the agricultural laboratories at the college three miles from town, and his white-collar optimism was catching.

But for Helmer, the moment of truth arrived in every job interview when his education level—ninth grade dropout—stopped the conversation. No amount of showing off his vocabulary, the amount of news he assimilated every day, his splendid if self-directed idiosyncratic breadth of knowledge. His factory experience from the northern city where he once lived, before Everett persuaded him to come south, "try a small-town atmosphere." Now only a bubble of disbelief that he could possibly fail so badly kept him going. After a while of this the interviewers were also smelling early morning liquor on his breath and cutting the talks much shorter.

"No thanks. We're done here. Frankly, we're completely done." Firm don't-come-back look. After each disappointment, he walked home, car-less in a sprawling town with no public transportation. Certain he had somehow swallowed a small round cactus that made his esophagus ache all the way to the roof of his mouth.

The apartment he shared with Ellen and their daughter was bleak and ill-made. "It's temporary," he told his wife. "As soon as I have a regular job, we'll move." He thought he would like the adventurous spirit of a small southwestern town and he tried to fit into the cowboy atmosphere, buying a pair of boots and a silver-plated belt buckle.

The first summer they lived here, the town had a Centennial Festival, and he took Janey to the parade, stepping over horse-dung piles of firm irregular balls still smoking and laced with green hay, as they crossed the street, and then to the fair grounds to munch buffalo burgers while watching the jalapeño eating contest. Janey felt sympathy as Helmer had challenged her to such a contest a few times, father and daughter stubbornly swallowing the burning green fruits until neither of them could see for the tears.

Several weeks prior to the festivities he had carefully nurtured a goatee til it hung free from his chin in a neat triangle exactly balanced by his sweeping moustache, and he boldly entered the "Buffalo Bill Look Alike Contest," even though this required an entry fee. "There's a cash prize, and I'm certain I will win," he reassured Ellen, who had to agree that he looked handsome, even distinguished. But on centennial judgment day his moustache just did not measure up.

"Not thick enough in the center," the judge told him when he protested at being placed fifth, "especially right under the nose." The old man waggled his yellow-nailed fingers close to Helmer's face, who resisted the urge to snap out with his teeth and draw blood.

Ellen fortunately had found a modest job that kept them from being evicted. She worked the counter at a drycleaners just off Main Street, taking in dirty clothing, writing down receipts, making small clothing repairs, being cheery with the customers. The chemicals from the back room gave her headaches, made her sneeze. For a while she became obsessive about washing her hands, which made Helmer nervous. But Ellen liked her job, she appreciated cleanliness, and interactions with people at such a basic level gave her a sense of connection to the town.

Whenever she would pass customers on the street, though they seldom recognized her, she noticed especially certain details in the states of their clothing, the careful crease in the pants that she had put there, the lace front she had sewed back in place on a blouse following the owner's particularly raucous vacation. As time went on, she knew much about the customers who brought their laundry to her counter. She knew which doctor vomited all over himself on weekends, and who had semen on the top covers of the bed when her husband was out of town. She was aware of which old man regularly shit his pants, which elegantly dressed four-year-olds had attended a particular birthday party, and which silent teenagers were drawing red lines up their arms with sharp instruments. She looked closely at the blood she occasionally found on women's clothing, not only at the inside crotch but more sinisterly at the collar, down the front of the delicate blouse, split lip sort of blood. She saw these women on the street as well and had her own thoughts about them. She looked closely at the faces of the men who sometimes accompanied them, comparing them to her Helmer, and he came out a winner.

If only he felt that way about himself. He was disappointed in his inability to find a job he wanted, and expressed this as chronic dissatisfaction with his choice of town. "Everyone is sloppy, they do shoddy workmanship here," he complained to Ellen. He said this so often she began to think what this meant to him.

For the craftsman there is an absolute truth, a trueness of the bore's diameter, an exactness of the setting of the lathe to one-sixteenth or one-thirty-second of an inch, the adjusting of angle of the carpenter's mitre to precise degree, and the evenness of the table legs sanded equally smooth to enable the level to pass the table top as truly parallel to the flat ground. Helmer's level was blue metal with a long glass eye on top, into which the user peered to check a flow of golden oil inside the glass. The top of the oil made a moveable straight line, a bit of magic.

Here in this new land the economic ethos was farming, or shop keeping, or ranching. Absolute truth of measurement wandered around according to some season—dry, lean, wet, a drop in sales and then a surge at Christmas time, cows in heat restlessly breaking through a fence. Solutions came through praying to God and the sky for water, gathering in community for support, keeping chickens in the back yard, walking the irrigation canals at night with shovels. Not whether or not the walls and doorways lined up perfectly straight or the culvert under the road stayed fixed.

When after six weeks the white-collar jobs crept further and further beyond his reach, Helmer found a job as a cook, "Temporary," he told Ellen. At first this was a fry cook, a short order cook, then he worked his way up to family restaurant jobs, then back down to short order cook, providing small town versions of fast food—the big chains hadn't arrived yet—cheeseburgers and fries, onion rings, pancakes with square pats of margarine and watered down syrup served in little white jugs.

The restaurant business shifts and twists like the body of a rattlesnake. Looks like it's going uphill and then skitters to the side, and down. Uneasy on the whimsical sands of public appetite and fad, health inspections and great skilled workers who suddenly move to another town to care for their parents or escape a DUI charge or avoid immigration snatching.

In the northern city he had belonged to a union and helped fight for worker's rights and union wages. He tried to talk about this to the waitresses and cooks at his jobs. They laughed. "They've never even heard the word 'union' here," he grumbled to Ellen. "This town is hostile to workers, downright medieval."

Family-owned businesses go under easily, and loyalty is a factor in their survival. Helmer gambled by continuing to work for old Mr. Hobbs three months without pay before the doors finally closed on a debt that could not be paid. "Only yourself to blame for that one," he said to his image in the bathroom mirror. His disappointments now were relentless stings, mounting into a throng of bullies inside him, as he began getting fired from one job after another.

Helmer treated all the objects he owned with meticulous care. He did not own many. In the living room his collection of perhaps twenty small books were packed neatly into the three-shelf mahogany bookcase behind his chair. His measuring calipers lived in a blue cloth-lined black case in the upper right-hand drawer next to the mirror against the west wall of the tiny bedroom. He showed them to Janey, taught her how the caliper could draw the circumference of a perfect circle and explained that he had used them in his factory job in Chicago as well as in his wood carving and metal casting, to measure precisely the diameter of various objects. His wood carving tools, including the tiny drills with the handles he had made, were stored in an open cardboard box under the bed. In the top right-hand drawer of the dresser on the east wall he stored his two dark antique pistols, which the daughter was forbidden to touch, and so of course played with frequently and with much enthusiasm when neither parent was home.

Against the wall by the closet stood his deer rifles, two of them, a Remington and a Springfield, whose wooden stocks he would rub with soft cloth saturated in linseed oil for hours on end. He had made the stock of the thirty-ought-six himself and whistled softly through his teeth while he did this meditative oil massage of the gleaming blonde wood. The whippoorwill song, "I'm So Lonesome I Could Cry," by Hank Williams, suited his mood of disappointed isolation. The musk smell of linseed and the sharp petroleum smell of gun oil permeated his territory, along with cigarette smoke, black coffee, leather, sweat, whiskey, beer, and frying bacon. Those were his smells and he loved all of them. They drenched the air in the apartment, which turned gunmetal blue with the swirls of his cigarette smoke whenever he was home, and awake. The blue swirls were like spirit dancers in the air around Helmer's chair, expressing the shapes of his breath, his ever-changing desires, his dissatisfactions.

On New Year's Eve that first year, he got drunk, and went outside into the front yard near the cinderblock wall, carrying his thirty-ought-six Remington rifle. There, sometime close to midnight, he pulled the bolt, threw a bullet into the chamber, lowered the barrel and blew a wide hole in the earth, the explosion making the requisite noise to satisfy his sense of renewing the year.

Helmer described himself as a nihilist, finding meaning and moral value in none of society's institutions, especially government and religion. When he brought up Kierkegaard or Ivan Turgenev, the Russian novelist, or even John Steinbeck, none of the other coworkers had any idea what he was talking about. They liked discussing sports and films, and he never participated in these discussions.

He did like to talk about song lyrics, especially one particular song that could be taken as satirical . . . or not. "Irene, Goodnight " is a farewell lament over an estranged relationship, a Leadbelly song written by Gussie Lord Davis in 1886, that had made it into the mainstream. Seeing your lost love in your dreams is benign enough in the chorus, but the verses are more sinister, telling a tale of a marriage on the rocks after just a few days. Helmer was amused by these lines, saying "See what I mean about this song being satire? It has to be a really BAD marriage to break up in less than a week." Sometimes his listener, someone sitting at the lunch counter, or later in the evening, a bar on Main Street, agreed, which encouraged him to continue, "And is it Irene who takes the 'stroll downtown'? Is this like she's already fishing for another husband? Is it a reference to the occupation of prostitution maybe? She's a lady of the night really?" This usually brought silence in the listener, who would change the subject, uncomfortable that someone as obviously aggrieved as Irene, the abandoned wife, could be considered an illicit person. Uncomfortable too that Helmer could not say "whore."

Now, after going through his third humiliation of getting fired, his fantasies turned increasingly to hunting. He imagined being one of those men who has a rack of guns in the dining room, and racks of antlers high on the mahogany den walls, dark glass eyes of the mounted heads catching the firelight from softly burning ceramic, gas-fueled logs along with the admiring eyes of a bevy of friends, cuddling brandy glasses and reminiscing about the hunts, the travels, the wars, the triumphs. But almost no visitors came to the little stucco apartment of his reality.

Ellen suggested he needed to belong to some group of guys who go hunting. He asked around repeatedly about this, at the bar on Hadley Avenue, and at work. However, as one of the night shift short order cooks finally told him, "Look, the guys who go hunting don't hang out with cooks." He tried to use Helmer's more formal language: "They just don't *consort* with us, get it? They are ranchers, or chamber of commerce types." The other cooks didn't have cars either. They didn't even have rifles, though one newly hired fellow had a beautiful set of carving knives that he brought to his job, as though he was a chef and not a fry cook.

"What does he do with his fine knives then," Helmer sneered to Ellen. "Chop up hot dogs before putting them on the grill?" He snorted, but she noticed that he was losing his sense of humor, and his goodwill toward others.

"What I most need is a car," he thought. Then he could expand his job hunting, maybe even organize a deer-hunting trip himself, break the class barrier. Pack the car with good-natured men and beer, drive into the mountains. Tell competitive jokes around a fire. Breathe air washed in pine tree sap, follow step by step behind broad shoulders and sure feet, plunge off on a path of his own. See antlers moving through brush. Stalk. Aim. Drive slowly back through town with the great heavy tan and brown body tied across the hood, enormous rack of antlers bobbing on the narrow head as it lobs off the side, near the fender. Nod with dignity to the people on the sidewalk who stop to look in admiration.

One day he called Ellen outside to witness his acquisition. A tow-truck had just dropped off the car he had bought for a few dollars, won in a card game. She saw immediately that it was rusting at the edges, had four flat tires. "Oh," she said, in her usual understatement, her face registering consternation. She knew he was no mechanic.

"The engine doesn't work yet, but that will come."

Nothing came though, not even a set of wrenches, as Helmer was increasingly pulled to spend all "extra" money on liquor, and the card luck, which after that one outburst, rolled over and lay still. The car hulked outside his apartment, sullen, windows down, an abandoned wounded beast. The daughter Janey, now eleven, soon moved into it as her "room." Spurning her former tomboy ways, she boldly fashioned pink pleated material as curtains for the side window spaces; they fluttered vividly in the wind, which made her father wince.

"One thing can be another thing," Ellen said when he expressed distress that their daughter had made her own space out of his shipwrecked car. She was thinking how she knew this from sewing, making pillowcases and an apron out of her old dresses. From cooking too, making cookies from leftover porridge.

But Helmer remained embarrassed at what his daughter had done with his prize.

Though Helmer could not find anyone to take him hunting, and had failed at gaining a car, he did have an adventure one Sunday. A young man, an Iranian engineering student at the college, had started coming in for lunch twice a week, after his trigonometry class. Introducing himself as "Amir here," he began a conversation. He liked that Helmer would specially grill the onions for his hamburger even though it wasn't a choice on the menu. Helmer liked that Amir had a moustache, like himself, and responded to his vocabulary with a fine one of his own. On slow days the cook would emerge from the broiling heat of the kitchen and sit at end of the counter, talking to any customers within reach. Amir began to sit down at that end, so a sort of friendship developed, one limited by the fact that Amir would return to his own country after June graduation in just a few months.

One day Helmer asked, would Amir take him hunting? No, the serious-faced Iranian replied, he didn't want to go shooting. "I want to build things, not kill them," he said, coming perilously close to insulting Helmer. Seeing the narrowing eyes on his friend he hastened to make an offer. There was something similar he did like to do, he said, just across the border forty miles away in Juarez. He invited Helmer for his next occasion, on a Sunday afternoon.

"We have to get there by three," Amir said.

The two drove in Amir's black ford, parked in El Paso, crossing the international bridge over the Rio Grande River on foot, and walking several blocks through a business district thick with people and the smells of frying tortillas, red chili, cumin, and bell peppers, past shop-keepers insisting on drawing attention to their carved green soapstone or silver cast candlesticks, and on to the noisy, crowded coliseum. A brass band in big-brimmed black Mexican hats was already blaring the entry anthem by the time they got to their seats on the benches over-looking the broad dirt arena with its ring of red panels like a painting of boundaries with blood.

On this particular day, there were six bull fighting events. So Helmer had plenty of time to ruminate on the occasion. His own impulse was to bet on the outcomes; however, bull fighting is a ritual of sacrifice, not a gambling opportunity, as Amir pointed out.

"It's the triumph of the sun king over the moon king."

"Do you have anything like bull fighting in your country?" Helmer asked. He had never known anyone from Iran. Amir told him about the Nowruz Persian New Year's festival in spring, how much fun it was, how much good food was cooked, the tons of delicate roses. "No animal sac-rifice though." He laughed, "Just a sheep at weddings—and that's only in the countryside anymore." He laughed again. "The women love the roses best, but the men love to kill sheep!" He did not say that the roses trailing from the headline of a colorful bull fight poster were what had first brought him to the coliseum. Then he had become fascinated by the matador's dance of life and death.

The matador had made a few passes with the bull, and now the toreros rode out, playing their more minor role in the drama, yet still elegantly dressed in black and silver, while the clothing of nearly all the matadors was lined in gold. All were impeccably dressed, their whole demeanor expressing graceful elegant courage to the crowd. The picadors had a more stolid appearance as they guided their horses into the ring. Their role is to poke the bull with their iron-tipped pics, leaving neck and shoulder muscles bleeding. Their horses wore thick long yellow blankets as padding, protection from the raging horns seeking to disembowel.

The more engaged Helmer became in the drama, the more he focused on the bull's fascination with the moving cape. Meanwhile Amir watched the studied posturing of the matador and explained the moves to Helmer. "Look how he gets the bull to charge and miss and then, look how he drops the cape to his side and just turns his back."

Amir cheered along with the rest of the crowd. "The bull just stands. The horsemen have lowered his head, see?" He applauded and sang out, "Olé!" He leaned toward Helmer. "He lowers his head more now, see? The picadors have weakened his muscles and his head drops. Then the warrior comes in with his thin sword, so thin, and ssssssst! Right behind his neck, into his heart." Helmer watched all this pageantry, heard the trumpets with the Spanish heraldry, smelled the dusty sweat excitement of the arena full of people, but he was transfixed by something else.

The angrier the bull became, the more he threw himself at the matador's cape, which in the third and final act of each bull fight, was small, achingly small, and red as a heart, the manoleto, yet still enough cloth to hide the gleaming thin sword. Finally, the moment of kill.

Helmer was mesmerized by the bull's insistence on rushing at the cape as if it were flesh he could engage. "He never gets it," he said to Amir, after the third fight. "He never gets that the cape is a ruse, a distraction."

"A bull is like a stubborn man, or a man in a trance." Amir responded. "The cape is his only desire."

"And yet," Helmer responded, "the cape is a complete illusion. The man is the reality." This point interested Helmer more than any other part of the drama, more than the heavy picadors or the nimble men jabbing pairs of multicolored banderillas to hang like long trembling darts from the bull's shoulders. The fixation of the bull on the flashing cape caught his attention more than matador number four who was a blonde woman named Betty, and almost more than seeing matador number six thrown high in the air over the bull's back, gored in the upper thigh, so that a few days later his leg was amputated, as Amir, who kept up with all the bull fighting news from the Juarez coliseum, reported later in the week over the lunch counter.

"The poor guy has lost everything," Amir finished. Helmer grunted in appreciation of the sacrifice.

Then it was June. Amir graduated, dropped in at the café to say goodbye, left Helmer a postcard with a picture of the Juarez bull ring, and returned to Iran.

After two years of getting nowhere with his attempts at a middle-class job, Helmer sometimes stared for long moments at the wall. He was looking at the road of his life ahead, and himself standing in a khaki uniform, holding a spatula, cursing at the grease spatters on his hand. Lately he had lost his taste for food, which had once been such a pleasure. Burgers, hot dogs, pancakes, even battered onion rings and grilled onions—his specialty—sickened him. At work he tasted none of the menu items, just sucked the secretly stashed vodka or whiskey bottle. At home he cooked for himself, and then only two strips of bacon and fried eggs. A little pepper on the eggs, black specks riding on the golden sea of broken yolk. Nothing else comforts him, except the song that has continued to catch Helmer's attention, he craves it repeatedly; gives the waitresses change to play it on the jukebox.

"Can't we throw Irene back in the river now?" one says sarcastically.

"No, play it again. And that's not the story anyhow." Whistles along while he breads chicken, adjusts the temperature of the boiling oil that will turn ordinary onions into tender delicacies. The lyrics played on in his head with their demand for the singer to stop his immoral behavior, and rhyming "rambling" with "gambling." But that's just what Helmer wanted to do: stay out late at night and do something that felt good. That would help him slow down his drinking, which had lately accelerated to an eighteen hour a day habit, with accompanying shaky hands and sideways gait.

He had begun taking sly looks at Sheila Ferguson. For six months he had worked with the blousy, easy-bodied red-headed waitress who was ten years younger than he and much more agile than you might think. Helmer knew this because her body motions revealed both her shape and suppleness through the fabric of her uniform. Soon he was watching a lot. He even liked the smell of her sweat, little tendrils of flowery acid curling toward him through the greasy stink of the grill. Though she had a loud voice that could be intimidating, he began to think instead about her hair, how it would billow out once freed of the net she, like all the waitresses, wore. Her loose hair would look both wild and vulnerable. Her voice, nothing like Ellen's soft placating tones, would, in the framework of his imagination, yield its aggression into a slightly hoarse and sexy alto, irresistible.

Soon his fantasies deepened: she would be attracted to him. He might even have a sort of affair with her. She would flirt for a couple of weeks, turning to smile with a plate in each hand, deliberately stooping to grab napkins from a lower shelf so he could see the backs of her legs, and higher. One day—no, soon—she would invite him, drive him in her blue Chevy coupe to the liquor store at the edge of town; they would sit together in the front seat, tell jokes and share a half pint of whiskey. He would be particularly witty, which she would appreciate with easy-going laughter. Then, looking at him sideways, she would nod toward the motel across the street, its vacancy light blinking an intriguing rose color . . .

He jerked, hearing his name. "Helmer!" Started his turn from the wide stove toward the open doorway leading into the table section. Sheila's eyes were flaming and she was moving fast.

"You son of a bitch! These are cold! The center is runny!" She balanced a plate of food in one hand. "Take them back and do it right this time!" His turning head was just in time to catch a stack of pancakes in the face, then awareness of the thick white plate bouncing hard off his boot, of syrup running like something childish on his cheek, and under his nose. The glare from her eyes sent a short stab to his heart.

Ellen had waited up most of Saturday night, sat tight-lipped as he closed the door meekly behind him. Last night local police had arrested him for disorderly conduct, held him in the drunk tank Saturday night, released him to stumble home on Sunday morning. He couldn't look at her. An urge had been growing irrationally within him, an urge to just take up his rifle, load the magazine. Stalk, aim. Shoot.

The Irene song was in his ears all the time, running at double, triple speed. Now a different verse, one revealing of the song's sinister meaning, as the singer declared that no matter where he lived he was haunted by his "great notion" to drown himself. In that same river the waitresses had joked about throwing Irene into. Weaving home from the bar one night, he sang the words to the sky; and when he reached home, finally as she emphatically questioned, he told Ellen how despairing he felt.

The next day she packed a cardboard box to move all the knives out of the house, the antique pistols too that she wrapped meticulously in paper after lifting them from the right-hand upper bureau drawer, and even her own pair of sewing scissors. She hid the lethal box in the shed downstairs. The two yellow boxes of ammunition she carefully carried to the back alley where the trash cans stood. She thought that if he wanted to blow off his head, leaving her with the loss and the ghastly theatrics of cleaning brains off the wall, he needed to very consciously go to the local gun store and buy a box of ammunition knowing exactly what he would use it for.

An hour after this Ellen firmly took her daughter's hand, suitcase of clothes in the other, and moved in with a neighbor woman. His wife moving out startled Helmer in his gloom and gave him space for thinking. He thought hard for two days and when a different song arrived on his whistle, he knew he had made a decision.

He remembered something he said to Amir on the drive back from the bull ring that Sunday evening. Speeding along on the dark road, they had been talking about pride, the pride expressed by the matadors' postures.

"And by the bull too," Amir added. "That they must lower his horns. He's like a great king standing on a high hill, and they must bring him down."

Helmer said, "A man's pride—a woman's as well—will do well by him until some moment when it becomes a raging animal within, bent on tearing out the very liver of its owner. That animal cannot be diverted; it must be fed something that satisfies, or it will rip loose like a pack of hyenas." He said this all in one breath to be sure to get it all out and took another slug from his bottle.

"Well said," Amir responded. "And who can be wise enough *soon* enough to say what that is?" He himself didn't drink though he also didn't seem to mind that Helmer was polishing off a pint of whiskey, undertaken earlier in the afternoon.

Ellen had stopped by the apartment every day on her lunch hour to check on her husband's emotional state, and to judge when it would be safe to move herself and her daughter back in with him. On Sunday, when she was not working, her daughter Janey, given to histrionics lately, dashed into the neighbor's living room with her mouth going off like a burglar alarm. "Ohhh ohhhhh Mom, Mom! I think he's done it!"

Ellen jumped out of her chair, hands to her face. "Done what?"

"The whole place stinks," Janey continued, her eyes enormous. "An awful stink coming from inside."

Ellen raced like a rabbit to the front door of their apartment, opened the door gingerly, crept inside. "Helmer?"

The stench was so strong she felt coated in it. Tiptoeing, her heart thundering, though rationally speaking, she didn't think blood would smell like *this* rotten, fat-dense, cartilaginous, glue factory sort of emulsion in the air.

Following a bubbling noise, she found his big stainless-steel stockpot simmering hard on her stove, a river of gaseous steam pouring from under the lid.

"Helmer! What *is* this?"

She heard whistling, then saw him sitting on their bed, calmly sanding a piece of wood. His eyes had a merry glisten she hadn't seen for a long time. Her heart softened, though she still felt nauseous.

He told her then, about the bull fight, how he'd kept thinking about it, how the bulls kept jumping right at the sword hidden in the red red cape of their own rage, how he knew there was only one thing for him to do.

"Yesterday, I walked all the way out to the meat packing company, outside of town way up on the west side, I just followed highway 31. They gave me the horns for nothing, so impressed that I would walk that far," he finished, and returned to his sanding.

Ellen looked at him in silence.

"It must have been 113 degrees out," Helmer added. Ellen noticed that his moustache was showing gray at the edges and was trimmed back, waxing days long gone. She knew he would need the rest of his tools now, and that she and Janey would move back in that afternoon, stench and all. She sighed in relief, exasperation, and commitment.

Ellen thought about his long walk, how out at the meat packing plant on the west side of town, a bull had been shot on the kill floor, his body strung up by the back legs on a big hook; his blood drained and saved to be dried as blood meal and fed to rose bushes; his tough meat harvested to be pounded into cube steaks for sale at the local Safeway; his internal organs sold to the pet food factory; his bones, teeth, and hooves gone to be pulverized for fertilizer. His hide to go for boots, belts, hats, and vests.

And what of the bull's horns, his long handsome gray and black horns?

She thought how Helmer had walked miles to the blood and shit–smelling place at the edge of town, bargained for the horns, and walked home under the blazing sun with the butcher-paper-wrapped package held in firm grip. His expression as he told this was extremely determined.

Reluctantly, Ellen peered under the lid of his shiny stainless-steel stockpot, wherein he had set the horns to boil, to get rid of all the marrow and the scalp meat. The smell had already permeated everything, even their clothing, and the process would take a long time.

"Ick! Ick! Ick!" Janey, who had followed her in, protested. "I will never ever *ever* eat meat again. And that's a promise!" Ellen sighed, partly in empathic agreement and partly in the foresight she had of many squabbles at her kitchen table at night, as husband and daughter acted out their differing beliefs.

Ignoring Ellen's nauseated expressions, he boiled and boiled his prize for three more days. Then he flecked off and gouged out all remaining debris of earthly life, dried the horns for several days and brought out his sandpaper.

Now after polishing and oiling them, he mounted them on an oak panel, bought at the lumber store, hand-sawed and hand-beveled around the edges. He sanded and lacquered the oak, turning it dark amber in color. The horns now came into view as parts of a story about containment of power. They have a fourteen-inch spread; they are creamy white with long sharp black tips and a dangerous upward curl; they gleam as though light-struck on a mountaintop, or in a field or even a bull ring. "See how they shine?" Helmer exclaimed to Ellen, who by now had done all their laundry twice. "You can almost see your face in them."

He hung the panel on the bedroom wall, in the small space above the dresser, right next to a straight-backed chair used to contain a stack of hunting and fishing magazines. And though the wall was not tall, the presence of the graceful up-sweeping horns made it seem tall. Maybe someday his successful once-friend Everett, who had never been to Helmer's place, would come over and admire them. But if he didn't, Helmer didn't care.

Once the horns were handsomely fixed on the wall, something settled.

A new song began to play in Helmer's head, a Johnny Cash song about keeping a close watch on his heart, and his eyes open, as a pledge of sobriety and faithfulness to his love June Carter. "I walk a straight line too," Helmer thought firmly. Ellen looked downward, smiling to herself whenever he came to the punch line chorus, even though to a stranger watching it would not be clear whether Helmer directed the song to his wife, exactly, or to the horns sweeping sharply upward like something that had just at that moment torn its way through the wall over his head.

Rats at the Door of Love

Can I tell the difference between love and all the other emotions? That's the question that always comes up whenever I remember what happened between Marietta and me after we moved to the suburbs.

Like someone from a movie, a guy I double-dated with in high school had LOVE tattooed on the knuckles of his right hand, and HATE on the knuckles of his left, so he always knew where they lived. I don't know where on his body he might have tattooed FEAR but if I was decorating Marietta and me that year, I would have stenciled it on our foreheads.

We moved to the suburb of North Oak Valley soon after we got together, though both of us had been in neighborhoods for years where we were perfectly comfortable. That was before we met each other. We would have done fine in my old neighborhood, it was full of our flags and our kinds of shops, men and women who looked and acted just as we did. Marietta and I would have fit in, even though we two are from somewhat different backgrounds. We would have been comfortable enough. But we had the romantic idea that owning a house would clinch something for us, I especially had this notion, and pushed for home ownership as a method of tying the knot right from the start. And from the start, we were uneasy about how folks in the "burbs" would receive us. We had heard rumors of incidents, we just didn't know.

We didn't have long to find out. The second week we were there we woke to find a spit wad on one of the back windows.

Was this just kids playing around? The spit wad was awfully big for just play, all of them together must have needed to contribute their spit. And since we hadn't talked to any of the neighbors we weren't sure what these kids called "play." Marietta had heard that the suburbs were full of gangs of kids who ran around looking for trouble. "They are called 'Rat Packs,'" she said. The seventeen-year-old son of a friend of hers had been attacked late at night in Berkeley, coming out of a movie theater. His hunched and bruised body came into my mind the first week when a group of screaming kids ran through the back yard and something smacked against the back of the house. A grapefruit from one of our trees, as I learned when I got up the courage to go out and see.

The Bay Area is much too cool to ripen grapefruits; their fruits grow huge, bundled in thick skin against the cold, and their pulp is dry and sour. People plant them as ornamentals for the lush green of the leaves, and the former owner had put two of them against the back fence. They were pretty unless you got too close, when their two-inch spikes could really scratch a gardener who was out there imagining paradise and not paying attention to reality. I know because I ran smack into one of them in the middle of my forehead, and it bled for an hour, while I cussed the tree and all its ancestors for almost that long.

Everything in our yard had spikes or thorns, as my fingers noticed painfully during the first few weeks. We had chosen the house because of its high enclosing hedge and air of being secreted. We thought a love nest should have good walls. The spiky Mexican palm in the small front yard had seemed protective to us then, the variety of rose bushes strung along the wire fence was very romantic, and we bid on the house despite the protests of the realtor.

That house is no good, she said, explaining that it sat in a low area and collected moisture. And the roof was terrible, she said. The more she tried to discourage us the more sure we were that this was exactly the house for us. "She doesn't understand what we need," I said, and Marietta nodded vigorously.

Not even the mildew on the wall of the north bedroom dampened our initial high spirits, as we Ajaxed the whole house and applied new paint in enthusiastic slathers. "As soon as we can we'll take the kitchen wall down and put a counter in, we'll be so modern," Marietta promised. This shocked me, as I imagined any changes in the house we would surely decide together. Who did she think she was, running out ahead with an idea like this?

The second spit wad arrived a couple of weeks later, even more enormous, a big collection of sticky pulp on the south corner of the front window. It must have taken ten kids just to make the thing. We spotted it the second we drove into the driveway. I exploded in wrath even before I got out of the car.

"They can't do this to us!" I yelled at Marietta, who had turned stiff and silent. Seething, I waited until ten o'clock that night to go out to remove the still wet mess. Then I quickly walked to our next-door neighbors', and plastered it on their window.

"If those kids are doing that to us, they are damn well doing it to all of you," I muttered to the block in general. I gritted my teeth at all the quiet, ominous houses. Home again and washing my hands I felt better, felt I was looking out for our little family.

Marietta had joked about running for mayor of North Oak Valley as we were finalizing the papers and running back and forth from the city moving the last of our household furnishings by stuffing the back seat of the car with boxes and lamps. Once we were settled I had expected her to have neighbors for tea or talk over the back fence, or even go to a church social. She did none of these, instead sitting on the couch in her free time watching television or talking a mile a minute to me. "The people who live around here look sinister," she said. I thought so too. No one approached us, or smiled as we drove past. Maybe they were worn out but maybe also they were hostile to us, maybe they had been listening to propaganda against us.

In our first six weeks on the block only one person made a friendly gesture, a little girl who one Saturday morning came into the driveway, past the hedge which I was watering. She was carrying a large black cat or at least attempting to, her small hands gripping him around his chest under his front legs. His back feet dragged and bumped patiently along the ground as he hung limp in her arms.

"Want a cat?" she asked. "Mama says I have to give him away." I certainly didn't want a cat, especially a grown one. If I was going to get a cat I would start with a kitten. I had my hands full with the yard, as parts of the hedge appeared to be dying of drought and the climbing roses were overgrowing everything else I had planted along the side fence.

The next day the cat was coiled in a black mass in the front yard. Evidently he had been evicted. When he was still out there on the second day I took pity on him and offered some food. He was in a bad way, with a seeping abscess on the left side of his jowl. I brought some hydrogen peroxide outside and cleaned his wound, talked to him a little. Marietta didn't want us to keep a cat so I didn't invite him in. "Go find yourself a home, fella," I told him, optimistic that he would leave of his own accord.

Maybe he would have better luck than we had had in finding a friendly neighborhood. Because when we pulled into our driveway from work the next day we were sickened to find a dead rat lying on the new doormat outside, carefully placed on its side.

"Oh my God," Marietta shrieked, and leaned heavily on my arm, her body bending and sweat breaking on her lip in the weight of her terror. We stepped over the offensive message and sat weakly together on the rose-colored couch, our joint prize possession in the narrow front room. I was in such shock I could hardly talk, while Marietta could hardly stop. "It's some kind of warning to us! They hate us. Why do they hate us so much?" She moaned, "Oh, we never should have moved out here."

I got a wad of toilet paper from the bathroom to wrap my hand while I picked the body up off the mat by its tail and carried it through the house—Marietta hid her face as it passed—out to the garbage can. I washed my hands six times before fixing dinner though I don't know why I bothered, neither of us was hungry. I scraped my plate into an old bowl and offered it out the front door about ten o'clock. The cat was there all right, seeming to feel a bit more chipper and with no lack of appetite. Wish I could be an animal, I thought. Nothing to care about or worry about except whatever is right in front of you.

In the weeks that followed our lives changed. I spent my evenings peering out the front window every time a car passed, especially if it slowed down. Marietta took our names off the answering machine message and the mailbox, which made me feel I had disappeared. She also stopped complaining that I was feeding the cat; she seemed to welcome any bit of life in our tender household. We clung together. "This will pass," she said.

She brought home a box of candy, held the rows of chocolate out to me; this was irritating, as I knew the sugar would rot our teeth, and had been urging her to eat fruit instead. When I brought this up again, she said bitterly, "Sugar is love!" and ate the whole box herself. It took a while, but we made up.

We went to the movies and were haunted by images of Nazis killing a Jewish woman's dog on the eve of rounding her up. Was that happening to us I wondered? As I began to like the cat more I also feared more for his life. And ours. Marietta had told me how neighbors of her folks were attacked by the KKK during the Great Depression, how they had a cross burned on their lawn. My folks came from a line that had been forced out of their country after a military coup and were still fighting mad. So the two of us together could hardly be the most relaxed couple—could we?

But we were hardly together, these days, hardly a couple. I could barely remember that we had talked about "all our lives" and even about getting married—before we moved to North Oak Valley. Now we never made love anymore, did not even talk deep into the night. Marietta's constant expressions of fear made me nervous and angry. She talked and talked, probing into my feelings. I withdrew.

I had always felt like the protective, heroic one and now it seemed she was looking at me as someone who couldn't take care of her. And why did it always have to be me? I began to resent her looking to me for heroism.

How could I be heroic if I couldn't find the culprit? What a sneaky, cowardly way to frighten people, I thought. My contempt for whoever had planted the rat spilled over into my other relationships as well, and I even began to dislike the people I worked with. What lay under the veneer of their friendliness I wondered. How would they feel about me living in their neighborhood?

So we passed the brief coastal winter, waiting for some other shoe to fall. The heater didn't work right either, and the man who came to fix it was—well who knew whether he overcharged us or not? Since it always smelled of gas fumes any amount he charged must have been too much, right? One day Marietta, without consulting me at all, went outside to instruct a delivery van. "I bought this for you Tammy," as the men carried in a yellow couch, and carried away our earlier couch. We had "picked it out together" though I don't care for floral patterns, but this new one was even uglier. She hardly left it anymore, sitting glued to the flowery cushions eating Danish buns and watching cop shows, which gave her nightmares.

I didn't like to go out in the yard anymore in case we were watched, and my lack of care made things worse since the hedge began to seriously die and anyone at all could see in through the barren branches. Then early in March the cat vanished for several days. I worried and fussed until he showed up one evening with his tail looking like a string of bubbles. All the fur was falling out, and the naked tail was riddled with tooth marks, each puncture swelling into an abscess.

Putting salve on him, I could just imagine how the cat had leaped a fence with a dog devouring him from the tail up. Maybe he had only managed to turn and claw his way free at the last moment before the teeth entered his gut. Behind this image was another, that of a gang of boys siccing their big German shepherd on my cat. On *my* cat in particular. "They could have done this one, too," I said to Marietta, and then tried to give her a comforting hug but she pulled away and looked down. I felt ashamed that I couldn't protect us.

The cat's injuries had not endeared him to her past that first outburst of sympathy. She now called him "rat cat," rather sardonically, as he continued to lose fur from his tail, and to lose weight all over his body from the strain of the abscesses. His injuries slowly responded to the antibiotic salve and as I applied it he purred against my hand and looked me in the eye. At least someone around here thinks I'm good for something, I thought.

One Saturday morning when Marietta was out I opened to a knock on the front door. A short stout woman looked into my face and said, "Well, you don't look like an axe-murderer!" I took a step back.

"Hi," she continued and told me her name. "I'm your next door neighbor."

Recovering, I invited her in, then made cups of coffee. We sat at the little table off the kitchen. She told me she was married, had two kids, felt restless, wanted to be a stand-up comedian in clubs in San Francisco. I told her as little as possible, but did manage to ask about the spit wads on our window.

"Oh those kids," she said, "they do that to everyone new."

After the neighbor's visit I thought things might settle down, but the last shoe dropped soon after the last abscess on the cat's tail stopped draining, just when I felt that the cat, at least, was recovering so maybe there was hope for the rest of us as well. Marietta and I were late for work on a Monday morning when we opened the front door to run to the car.

"Look," she said hoarsely, and didn't say another word for about an hour. On the mat was the second rat, a bigger one this time, and not a bit stiff-looking. A fresh rat, carefully arranged so we would see it. Riding together on our long commute we didn't once turn our faces to the other one, and she didn't lay her hand on mine on the steering wheel except to give me the daily dollar for the bridge.

That night I don't even know which of us exploded first. I just remember a lot of crying and some screaming and broken dishes. Then we fell into each other's arms. "Let's take care of each other," we said, "we can make it through if we just hold onto each other tight enough."

For a while this outburst brought us closer together as we struggled up from the depths of our terror. "I just want to be like other people, I just want to fit in," Marietta wept against my chest.

"I just want everything between us to be like it was last year," I mourned. In our last neighborhood we hadn't fit in either, but people had looked up to us as leaders; we were gregarious, had people over, fed them. I wanted to feel special like that again.

But it was useless. Everything continued downhill. If she brought me a present I thought she was bribing me to be nice; and the more I cleaned and carried out the trash and cooked the more imperious she seemed, as though I was just her servant. We bickered all the time, until no love light shone from our eyes. I dreamed I was chasing a rat to hit it with a club, but it hid under the car; I couldn't find it. I woke chilled.

Through the dullness of my heart during those months I noticed an old robin who came that spring to build his nest in the taller of the two grapefruit trees. All through March he waited for his love to arrive; she never did. I saw him out the kitchen window nearly every day, prowling on the fence or the grapefruit tree. You could tell he was old because his cheek feathers were gray, and his wing and back feathers were worn and broken. He was a big, slow, proud looking bird, and I identified with him. Not that I am old, far from it, just that I too had built a nest for my love, I too was waiting for love to arrive. The first week of April he gave up and left.

In June so did I.

Marietta shredded my favorite shirt, put the house on the market and moved in with an old lover.

I called her a bunch of ugly names that she would never forget, grabbed my stuff and dropped the cat off to board at the nearest veterinarian hospital off some freeway exit I barely noticed, and then kept driving. I spent two weeks on the road trying to understand my life, and when that didn't work I came back to the Bay Area. I got another job.

My new apartment was in a neighborhood I knew. At least I felt comfortable enough to breathe again, though I was sorely missing something. I figured it was too late but then one afternoon I just went ahead and got on the freeway headed toward North Oak Valley and was fortunate to guess the right exit. Even though it had been eight weeks the vet remembered me, and gave me an icy look. The cat was still there, lying in the cage too depressed to look at me and with that snuffly little cold they always get in those places.

The lease had been specifically clear, "no cats" so I sneaked him to the second floor up the back stairs. I took him into the kitchen, showed him his bowls and then turned him over and tickled his belly. "I'm not going to leave you any more," I promised. He began to purr again. Since he'd never lived in an apartment I made an agreement with him to carry him down to the front door and let him out whenever he wanted.

This worked for about a week until Saturday afternoon I was painting the middle room peach to match my new shirt when I heard the most unbelievable yowling and moaning. I couldn't locate the sounds at all at first, even sticking my head out my front window, and then going down to the front door. Finally I went outside and peered up into the tall cypress tree that stood against the building. There halfway up was the moaning cat, trying to make it to my open window, unable to maneuver any higher through the narrowing upper branches. I called him and he took a chance and jumped down on me, and I immediately saw—and smelled—the reason for his racket. His whole back half was coated in old gunky motor oil, and now, so was my new shirt.

As I carried him in, I saw some fellows next door working on their car, the oil pan sitting on the sidewalk. The cat had fallen into it. I knew it had been an accident because I had seen him making friends with them all yesterday evening on my way home from work.

I soaped him several times in the bathroom sink and toweled him for a long time to get the thick goo off. I wanted him to eat the least possible amount of petroleum when he finished the cleaning job himself. He seemed pleased with my job, and, confidence restored, was back outside with the mechanics almost before his fur was dry. That was fine with me. It was so hot the manager had propped the heavy front door wide open, and this also meant the cat could come and go as he pleased. I just hoped the manager didn't see him or care one way or the other.

I felt at home in this neighborhood, which I'd lived in for four years once before, and never with any kind of trouble. So I almost dropped the sack of groceries I was carrying when I came home from work the next evening and found a dead rat laid out on the mat in front of my apartment door. I was gasping for breath, as I set the sack down and leaned against the railing. I resisted the initial impulse to turn around and run.

I decided to use my head instead.

Then, I began to look at that rat. I must have looked at that rat longer than anyone has ever looked at anything. I looked at that rat longer than a long meditation or a long movie or a long dream. I looked at that rat all along the inside of my head, and through my whole relationship with Marietta, and everything that had happened in that suburb, and everything I knew about that cat.

When he came home that evening I had already taken rubber gloves and put the rat in the trash can downstairs, though if I'd known how to skin it and clean it and cook it up and sit and eat it with him I would have done that instead. I called him from my chair in the living room, and he came to sit in front of me washing the remains of his canned-food dinner off his black and white face. When I began talking, he turned his face up and I saw how golden his eyes were. I leaned down and touched noses with him in a family way. Then he was at the door ready to go downstairs again. I went with him, and he trotted right over to his greasy new friends. I gave them a wave.

The heart has its own literacy, could I ever learn to read it? If I could, the tattoo would be "Love" on the right hand, and "Love" on the left hand too. Poor old robin. He had to wait for his love, and she never showed up. My cat and I from now on we sit out on the front steps, talking to everybody. Actively seeking.

Bugs

My mother went crazy at the age of forty-six, and I guess it was her menopause although I'm not sure. She wouldn't talk about what was bothering her deep down, she just began to act differently. Very, very differently. Instead of filling the house as usual with the thick delicious smells of steak and potatoes, liver and onions, or bacon and eggs, she declared she was no longer eating meat.

My father went into immediate deep shock over this, meat being the central axis of his life. He spent his youth on a Colorado ranch supplying meat for his father's family in the form of cow innards and occasional sides of beef, in addition to game that he and his brothers brought back from their nearly weekly hunting forays. Deer, antelope, elk, teal, quail and rabbits graced the family table, and the smoker in the backyard was frequently busy preserving steelhead and other trout pulled from cold fast waters. My dad was fourteen when his own dad was killed on the front lines in Korea, and he took his family responsibilities very seriously. "Bringing home the bacon" was his byword, and when he had a chance to become a partner in a small meat packing firm, he took up the occupation without a second thought.

Now with my mom, whose name is Nancy, declaring her refusal to participate in what was the center of our family life, my father was torn between two powerful forces of morality. One said that eating meat was like praying, like living, and certainly like being sane, and the other said that he mustn't go against the woman's wishes under her own roof. The workplace and the public place were to be the man's, the house was ruled by the wife. This was how his father had taught him. As his only son, I was situated somewhere between as I wasn't yet grown and into my own dominion. I was fifteen when she began her episode by sitting down in the kitchen one evening and refusing to cook supper.

"I just can't do it, Marvin," she said in an unusually low, hoarse voice, "I just can't cook tonight, or any night. I can't eat meat any more, and I can't stand the smell of it cooking."

"She doesn't feel well," he explained to me as I sat puzzled in front of my empty plate. "It's her female thing, her change." I didn't know what he was talking about though. Since the girls at school seemed to change every other day. I thought he meant something about temperament.

I told my friend Frank at the end of the week, "My mother is having a bout of temperament. That's why she isn't cooking anymore." I didn't tell him that my dad had spent every night trying to persuade her to return to her duties, without avail. She sat in the living room in a rocking chair, and looked at the wall as she moved back and forth in the confines of her own orbit. "I don't want anything to be killed anymore, Marvin," she said.

Now that I know more, it's like she was saying, "If I can't bleed any more, nothing else can either."

"Look what she got at the store," my father said at the end of that first week in an undertone, as though we must not let her know we were discussing her activities, although she was sitting right there, rocking slowly, staring at the wall. He put an elbow under my arm to get me into the kitchen, showed me the tiny sack she had carried in from the car, and the three cans of kidney beans, the quart of milk, the box of dry cereal.

"This is what she is eating. Nothing else. You can see this is serious, son."

"What are *we* eating?" This was more to the point. We had gone every night to the fast food place, and then Dad broke down and took us out to eat for a sit down meal. He is cheap about restaurants, having a dinosaur notion that we should "catch our own dinner"—from where, the bridge over the new freeway?—but Friday night he took me out to Joe Swift's Steak and Lobster place and we indulged in prime rib, and he drank Jack Daniel's whiskey and had a hangover the next day. I think he was beginning to feel sorry for himself. In any case that was the last of Joe Swift. From then on he made a list and sent me to the store, in his car.

"Get back in one piece and within an hour," he commanded.

I did pretty well, only one little dent. I avoided Frank's challenge to a drag race and only drove past the new mall twice, my eye out for what us guys then called "quail" and I see now was just "young women's attention."

Most of what I bought was edible, at least it would have been if the two of us hadn't tried to cook it. My Dad could barbecue with the best of them. It was boiling water and measuring macaroni and flour that eluded his expertise. And, I quickly saw, he could not master the new glass top electric stove with its twenty separate though mysteriously related choices. My dad was a "big picture, big sky" guy. He could rope a calf from his early youth on a Colorado ranch and supervise butchers at his meat packing plant as they swiftly carved chops out of dressed and chilled half-carcasses. The stove—not so much. Sometimes the timer was set but not the burner; other times the burner melted the aluminum lining in silver drips out the bottom of the copper pan and sent us running to the sink to douse thick black smoke.

"That's it," he said in disgust, after I accidentally triggered the auto clean button and we could no longer open the oven door. "We're cooking outdoors from now on." After the first few nights of grilling burgers and hot dogs over coals in the backyard our neighbor Smith began poking his big-eared curious face over the fence asking where Nancy was, and that scared my dad. If there was anything he hated, it was invasion of privacy, and the idea that people would know his wife was strange in the head was more than he could bear.

He moved a little cast iron hibachi we had used for camping into the kitchen, set it right on the stove near his tongs and long spatula, and the hand-rescuing fire glove. We disengaged the smoke alarms while I controlled the smoke with a wet dishtowel and the smoke sucker fan on the stove. Dad would have me read some recipes to him, and then he would try to bring them to fruition, using frying pans over hot coals. My job was to pay attention to the timer, open the windows to chase the smoke out and scrub the bottoms of the pots with baking soda whenever they burned. And not make too many faces, like rolling my eyes or otherwise pointing out that this was all his harebrained idea. I would have settled for deli chicken potpies or frozen Mexican dinners. But Dad had a major superstition about freshness.

"Fresh meat is what this family gets," he insisted. Someday I will take him back to his ranch and show how it's been subdivided, and the only fresh meat is snails in the tiny lawns and young girls at the freeway exits selling sex for meth. But I sure was not going to say this to his face now.

Mom meantime, placidly ate her kidney beans and toast or bowl of cereal with a little milk. She didn't go out except brief walks to the store for carrots and beans after she gave up driving, just sat and rocked, and didn't talk to us. It wasn't as though she was mad, just not exactly there, with a small irritating smile curling her lips.

So we were doing all right, muddling through I would say, the food was terrible and the kitchen was always a mess, but we were holding on while she went through her phase, until the first cockroach showed up.

I noticed it first sauntering out of the silverware drawer, then found a bunch of little ones under the toaster, three, four, then zillions. Dad kept saying "Where, where?" as he had taken to leaving his glasses in his bedroom rather than coat them with grease from frying. "Several of them," I insisted. I was amused at their invasion. The babies—so shiny they looked enameled—ran fast, disappearing among the breadcrumbs, and scattering for cover in all directions when the toaster was lifted.

The bugs and our mess seemed totally out of place in the clean geometry of our kitchen, which my dad had designed when they remodeled and my mother had always kept meticulously clean, not allowing me to bring home a single pet. No dog trotted beside my bicycle, no hamster smelled of grain in his wire cage, no goldfish flashed in a bowl in the kitchen window.

I had hardly ever seen a bug, so fastidious was our family at keeping the house and yard sparkling clean. We did not even have germs or weeds, never mind bugs. We had enough bug killer in the garage to massacre every spider in the county. And now we couldn't use a drop of it.

Mom was adamant. "No killing, Marvin," she repeated firmly. "I won't have any more killing in my house."

"Does that include weeds in the carport?" I asked. "How about mold in the refrigerator?" For this he struck out bitterly in my direction with his voice, told me not to be sarcastic to my mother. I could hear from the hoarseness of his larynx that he was feeling seriously conflicted.

The roaches thrived, not only multiplied and left their shiny egg casings in all the kitchen drawers, they gained size dramatically. They took control of the air space. And this is where they left my amusement behind. A gang of them had taken to gathering around the light fixture in the kitchen, and these had wings. They circled the light for a moment after it was turned on, and then flew directly into my face. I yelled and ran the first time.

Then I tried the soldier-under-fire approach, shielding my face while I headed for the faucet for a drink. I was still at that age when drinking directly from the faucet is the only normal way to get water. Evidently the roaches thought this too, as several were on the faucet while others had gathered at the bottom near the garbage disposal. The sink full of moving bugs was sickening, so overwhelming I was dizzy, and turned away, wiping my mouth, wondering if I had swallowed one by mistake. The third time I completely forgot them, turned on the light and had a big flying roach land on my nose. I could feel its feet on my upper lip. I yelled and ran that time too, seething in the dark in my room for the next hour.

It occurred to me then that cockroaches were some kind of extension of my mother's mind. Thoughts she had never revealed. Something swarming around underneath that little smile.

"Carrots are so good for you," she said the next day when I tried to confront her with my frustration over conditions in the kitchen. She was sitting calmly in her rocking chair, eating a plate of raw carrots, carefully peeled and cut. For the first time I realized I was speechless before her; I could barely talk or tell her what was happening in the house. She smiled looking past me as I stuttered and failed.

"Want one?" She held out her neatly arranged plate.

"Mom, this morning I found a cockroach walking on my toothbrush with their filthy feet." What I wanted so say was, "We really *need* to kill them. And by the way, what IS the matter with you?" And I couldn't get the words out. All I could think was that the roaches never seemed to go near *her.*

"They're clean," she replied placidly. "We all live together in the same clean house." And returned her gaze to the wall.

I brought her condition up with Dad. "A psychiatrist, maybe?"

He shook his head sadly. "I promised her I would never do that," he said.

I didn't return to the kitchen at night. I skipped dinner and stayed in my room, as the little shining ones were beginning to show up in the living room as well. And finally they came into my room. I could feel them run across me in the dark. Then I frequently stayed awake with the covers over my head and tucked completely under me to lock them out, to keep them from actually walking on my body. I began to loathe especially the idea of them touching me, influencing me with their quivering, knowing me with their feet, investigating me with their antennae. Questioning my right to my own territory.

The last time I looked closely at one of them it had pale yellow cheesy stuff all up and down its arms. Legs, I guess I should say. Disgusting way to carry food around, like gluing it to your body. Though something about the way their legs had little protrusions to hold stuff, like a stack of shelves, caught my attention for one moment, architecturally you might say. Then I shuddered.

Not looking at them didn't help because I could still hear them, running across the plastic fibers of my down quilt. They made a minute whooshing sound as they displaced the air, and I became acutely, even supernaturally, skillful at detecting them. I frequently fell into a fantasy involving them. Perhaps I could be hired in some biology experiment, as a specialist in entomology. Answers only I had determined, would impact human-insect relations; I had deciphered their language, won their trust, and they were telling me secrets of how to save the rainforest. Meanwhile far into the nights my nervous ears recorded their sounds and movements, searching without result for meanings on the other side of my growing fear and fury at the restrictions in my life.

Roaches weren't the only life form that now ruled our house. Spiders with long skinny legs dominated the bathroom, and moths flew from the bread box in short powdery gusts. No one came over anymore, not even Dad's family. He would meet his nephews, sisters and their husbands at the motel when they came through town, giving some excuse about "Nancy's health." Or more remodeling. Mom, meantime, had taken off all her make up and now had too much of a glow to her cheeks and eyes. Madness, I thought, though she did look a lot less tired.

My dad looked exhausted. "I'm bugged here, I'm bugged at work. I'm thinking of selling the business," he confided one evening. What? Wasn't that the business I would someday inherit? He didn't say more, and I didn't tell him about my troubles. My problems in school began with language, I think. Repeatedly I asked my friend Frank to explain the assignments to me; I couldn't remember them. Nothing the teachers said made any sense, and the words on my computer screen appeared to be in a foreign language, and then not a language at all, just marks. Patterns, as meaningless to me as those made by the antennae waving across my quilt at night. Peering closely, I could now see that yes, the letters did look like individual insects, seeming to move incessantly, even to interact, yet without communicating anything, not adding up. I was filled with horror at the meaninglessness, that the center of the world had fallen apart, that life itself was just purposeless motions.

As the weeks passed, I fell deeper into a private hell. I had nightmares of giant roaches coming toward me, their huge black reflective eyes staring into mine. The kitchen light I no longer used for myself gleaming from their dark orbs. In the grocery store I could swear little ones were looking out at me from under the bananas and more than once several poked long antennae at me from between the oranges. They would pull back when I looked at them directly, and I hoped no one else had noticed them. I was sure I had brought them to the store from home.

Repeatedly during the day I jumped, slapping at my sleeve or getting out of my seat at school to yank off a sweater and shake it out. They were following me everywhere. I developed a tic at the corner of one eye and it's possible my mouth twitched as well. I had stopped looking in mirrors as I didn't want to see the roach I could feel wandering through my hair. I could hardly stand to comb it anymore. My friends disappeared, and so did my good grades. My lifetime dream of attending the best engineering program in the country, and of signing up for ROTC faded as I flunked class after class, unable to understand the exam questions. Unable to see past my quivering anxieties. The night after we took exams for special college prep classes and I couldn't make the letters form words I knew my life was wrecked.

One night I decided to talk personally to Frank; when I approached him, he invited me to spend the night at his house and we stayed awake till four, and I found the words. Dad had sworn me to secrecy over what he called our "mother problem" so it was a major decision to talk to Frank about what was happening.

"Your damned mother, she's nuts," he said vehemently, he was always loyal to me. I was deeply humiliated to hear him say this even though I agreed. "She's just a little buggy," I countered, "she's really a good mom."

I told him my idea that the insects were my mother's out-of-control thoughts.

"She's bug-nuts!" he laughed. "That's why they called that gangster "Bugsy Siegal—cause he was bug-nuts!"

"What?"

"Crazy. Completely." At this a wall broke inside and I sobbed. I hated this breakdown, it meant I would always owe Frank something. I could see from the grim set of his jaw that he blamed my mother for all my problems. I couldn't let Frank have such a huge piece of negativity about my mom. "She's not so bad, just this episode. She used to make me special apple pies and stuff." There, at least I had defended her.

This was my only satisfaction, because now things took another down turn.

All my life my father had promised to take me deer hunting. It ran in the family; deer hunting was like an initiation into manhood, more important to us than any of those stupid goldfish-swallowing, leave-you-naked-on-the-highway-in-February drunken fraternity things. We had planned the trip down to the last detail, studying the maps, marking trails. He had taught me to shoot at the rifle range, and how to test the wind out in the yard. I knew all about looking for spoor and reading the hieroglyphs of their tracks; and how to drop on one knee so I wouldn't tremble and misaim or freeze up on the first shot. With his permission I had invited Frank, secretly knowing this would be my time to shine, a time to make up for all of Frank's sports honors.

And now the hunting was not to happen. "I won't have it, Josh," she said firmly. "Killing is wrong."

This was the only time I begged her, and I saw how truly hard she was, how unmoving. My dad did not join in. He sat like gray cardboard, remote from us both. Only later did I learn that he had already decided to put the meat processing plant on the market. He had become depressed at work, and his employee morale was so low the company was sustaining injuries for the first time in its history. Paying out worker compensation was wrecking the company's foundations until the accountant had advised immediate sale.

Just before the final papers for the sale were signed my mother changed again. Even she seemed puzzled, however faintly, by this turn, as though whatever grand statement she had been making had simply slipped into thin air.

She woke up one morning with no more yearning to stop killing, and when she told my dad, he came to my room at once. "Go to the store and buy a big new can of Raid," he said. "She has lifted the ban on killing." We sprayed till our eyes burned; the stuff dripped from the ceiling and ran in chemical columns down the walls. I took special pleasure in watching the flying ones spin fast as though to speed away, flop crazily to the floor and turn belly up. Whole families staggered from the back of the silverware drawer and dropped into the sink. I sprayed into the flour and pancake mix until moths helicoptered into the walls. Then I chased spiders round and round the bathroom, watching their legs curl like fingers.

"Everything's normal again," I told my friend Frank. "Our house is like paradise. My mother is well. My dad didn't sell his business after all. He and I ate a big steak at Joe Swift's to celebrate. My mom ordered crab. Everything in our house is peaceful and quiet. The cockroaches are all dead." I was very excited. Now we could go on with our plans, we could engage with life. And by the way, I said to Frank, my mom's episode wasn't brought on by menopause, she just had a nervous breakdown.

"Oh wonderful," he replied. Frank had just been accepted to MIT. "How about you, did you get into the college you wanted?"

"I'm not going to college." I looked down at my shoes. "I'm going to trade school, going to have a career doing something I really *really* want to do."

"What's that?"

"Exterminator!"

We laughed, I laughed the hardest.

Frank did become an engineer and helped work on what became famous irrigation and desalination projects in places like South Africa and Dubai. But I didn't settle for "exterminator." I went back to finish high school, then on to study biology, and became fascinated with structures of shiny flying things. And the interspecies social engagements of ants, the language of butterflies, the reactions of honeybees to insecticides, and how they dance to talk to each other. I did the unexpected, and became an ecological entomologist. My mom is proud. My dad looked shocked when I told him, and then he laughed until tears ran down his cheeks.

Only Strawberries Don't Have Fathers

I've had to make my own jobs up ever since I got out of the hospital, the sixth floor ward, psych ward to be exact, so I wasn't surprised that nobody would hire me. That was OK, or at least it was familiar, "be resourceful" I said, and collected scrap metal around town and took it over to the junk yard down on second street, that's how you stay in cheese and bread. They had a dog there among the discarded car parts and cans, a supplement to the barbed wire on top of the fence, a Rottweiler who looked half starved so I shared my food. This worked out okay until one day the dog just went nuts, reminded me of my dad, and chewed on my arm, then it looked like a flute from wrist to elbow. Amazing regular red holes!

After a couple days my arm started to feel like it wanted to leave the material realm, well, I didn't want to go back to the hospital for anything, fortunately someone I knew on the street, my friend Hayscoop, told me about Dr. Darby, that she would treat poor people on the spot so to speak, so I hung out in front of her clinic for a few hours and after a while there she was. Noticing me. Tender eyes. Took a short look at my flute and invited me to her house; we got into her car together. Turned out she not only cleaned everything up and gave me a shot, she listened and then told me I could sleep in a little cottage in the back of her house while she took me through a course of rabies vaccinations in case I needed, even though I wouldn't tell her where the dog lived. Her house was a neat three-bedroom rowhouse on a 150-foot-long lot, with one of those delicious-looking two-story tumble-down cottages in back, built in the 1930s. Perfect for me, even a crawl space underneath stuffed with wild crabgrass where I could hide whenever necessary. First thing, I met her wife, Sarah, and their cat Morgan. Sarah held my flute arm just so while the doctor bandaged me.

To repay this ultra-spectacular kindness I became their gardener that very moment. Told Dr. Darby I could raise all the vegetables and fruits she and her wife Sarah could eat. They went inside their house to talk this over, which I could hear through the open window, and while they did I changed my name to Clovis. My dad would never find me with a name like that. Sarah said I could stay for a trial period if I would take a shower, comb my hair, and allow them to buy me some new clothes. Ho, I wasn't ready for all that but said I would do some of it if they would let me go get my cat Marmalade as I was missing her, and the not-always-reliable Hayscoop was keeping her on the street while I was in the hospital. So, more confab inside the house while I counted the different food garden spaces they were wasting with landscape plants, and decided where the compost pile should go.

I had a prescription and a bottle of meds from my last stay—in the hospital—but after a few weeks I just had a problem with those meds. Here is what I love to do: get to know creatures and plants, get the dirt wet with buckets of water and put my hands in it to stir it up, come upon a little tangle of earthworms down underneath, and look at their dark and bright red stripes like Scandinavian T-shirts. Then listen to the wind talking to me, especially at night. With these meds no matter how small I cut the pill, I felt dull, you can't feel dull in a garden, it begins to dislike you. You have to dance with the plants! And the wind lately wasn't saying anything interesting, as I kept forgetting to ask the questions. Lonely times like these, I stop taking anything, don't even eat, and it works out better. Until my dad comes after me and I need to hide.

It was during one of these times that Dr. Darby came back to the cottage yard to find me. By now I was sometimes calling her Dr. D., to myself. More intimate, don't you think? She peered at me under the house where I was curled into the crabgrass, had been there for a couple of days. She stretched out on the ground so we were on the same level. "What's up?" She picked a blade of flat onion top and sucked on it.

"My dad again," I said. "He came by on the street in his black pickup truck earlier. I know he's looking for me. He goes round and round the block. Until."

She moved the grass to the other side of her mouth. "I don't think your dad could drive all the way from Kentucky to this exact street, and find you," she said.

"Oh yes, I saw him. I've seen him lots of times."

"Well, we won't—Sarah and I would never let him take you. I hope you know that. And I will be on the watch for him. Now come on out."

I rolled out. Crabgrass, I had noticed, was crawling up through the floorboards on its way into my kitchen. Dismantling a house from the floor upwards. How creative!

"What's that blood on your arms and face?" Dr. D. asked, "Did you cut yourself?"

I licked my arm. "Strawberry!" I said. I had rolled right through my own carefully planted strawberry bed, and some were already fruited out. When I first planted the bed Dr. Darby had come out and read the plants' life story to me from the *Good Neighbors Gardening Newsletter*, delivered free twice a month:

"Strawberries don't have fathers. The strawberry plant, clumped with integrity into a short cylindrical body (the 'crown') seated on roots and enfolded by small, neatly defined deep green leaves, is a matriarchy. Though producing flowers which then convert to the luscious pointed fruits so dear to lovers of the sweetmeats of earth, the seeds are irrelevant to strawberry reproduction. Instead of mating and matching, the strawberry plant sends out root runners with probing tips which plant themselves and grow daughter plants complete in themselves, continuing the process until the strawberry bed is a dense matrix of parthenogenesis."

Strawberries don't have fathers but cats definitely do. Cats are matriarchal too as far as I can tell, and the way Morgan and her daughter incorporated fathers into their family is what I want to tell you about. Making a comparison of Dr. Darby's lesbian family with Morgan's cat family makes sense given that in both cases the question is, what is the experience of two mothers raising a baby who wish to turn its care at least partially over to a male of their choice? Because it turned out by the time I moved in, Dr. D. was pregnant.

Morgan had to be the smallest grown cat anyone has ever seen, jet black with yellow eyes, thin and vivacious. We became soulmates on first sight, and soon I had stolen her heart away from the women in the front house. She was about ten months old when she came to live with me, and very fast she went into heat for her first time, when boyfriends galore showed up to posture with each other in the back yard. She chose only one: Papa Cat, a small muscular guy who had the pretty orange, brown, and black markings of a Burmese. She loved him so much she brought him inside the front house to have sex under the big shiny dining room table. No one else being home, I followed them in and watched. As he pulled out, she shrieked and slapped him across the face, yet obviously she enjoyed herself and soon they were back at it. Later I learned that Nature—the strangest person I know—had set it up this way; his penis has a hook that scratches and causes her to release her eggs. For this alone I don't want to be a cat. Except sometimes.

I must say that dining room table came in for some multiple uses. That's where I had sat while Dr. D. swabbed out my arm, and that's where Sarah set the table with two lasagna-steaming plates for the two of them, and green cloth napkins. She loved cooking and food of all kinds, and she also loved to lay naked out on that dining room table while Dr. D. sat in a chair between her legs. I found this entertaining to hear while I puttered in the fern bed under the window, where I had planted garlic and onion bulbs, and have to say I love orgasms myself. I won't tell you where I get them from, though I will say it has to do with water. Anyhow, to get back to Morgan and Papa Cat, he stayed with her for weeks, sat with her on the back steps of the big house, ate inside my little cottage by her invitation, and left before she swelled all the way up. Then weeks later he returned for a short visit and she brought him into the cottage downstairs bedroom where she allowed him to see the babies.

The cat family became the Dynasty of Morgan as soon as I kept one of her daughters from that first litter. Leah (Leah-pard) was rabbit-brown and spotted like a leopard, with the deep apricot apron of her Burmese father, Papa Cat. Like him she had the feral fur of wild animals, each hair genetically painted with three colors, casting lights and shadings of camouflage across her body. She always looked as though she was tensely crouched in dappled sunlight falling through dense foliage. Her ears were sharply pointed with long spikes of black fur at the ends, like a lynx or a bobcat. Her personality was calm and removed, and unlike me who is always on watch she paid little overt attention to human beings. Her central focus was her tiny black mother.

My central focus is in case that truck comes to get me. My dad says that I am the kind of creature God does not like, and that everything bad that happens is all my fault. So naturally I have felt closer all my life to other creatures God does not like. Number one is earthworms. My dad hates them, says they are little snakes and a snake ruined life in the First Great Garden. But I know that no garden does well without worms, they make the plants prosper, and besides they outnumber human beings by a bazillion to one. So if the garden loves them, I love them.

I love them even more now that I have learned they are androgynous, they aren't men or women, each one is both, yet they don't mate with themselves, instead fall in love with each other and mate for the longest time you can imagine, hours and hours, think about this in worm time: days, even years, of continual bliss. I love them so much for this! I just wanted to be near them so crept out quiet about midnight where I found two of them in the ground cover, on their honeymoon, slick with mucous, shiny and perfect. They were facing opposite directions, each one balanced in the saddle of the other. I have never even imagined such perfectly executed love. So I covered my eyes with a bandana, in honor of them not having eyes, and laid down as close as I could without bothering them.

I was lying out there like that one night on my back, feet splayed out, as still as a dead rabbit when suddenly I heard, "Clovis, what are you doing?" and sat up in a whirl. There was Sarah with a flashlight, gave me such a start, at first I thought my dad had surely found me. But right away I had to reassure her that I was okay because I guess lying on the ground at night was strange to her.

"You can c-c-come out Clovis, it's Sarah," she said, as I had rolled under the cottage into the crabgrass cave.

"I know," I said, "everything's fine." Hoped I hadn't crushed any of the baby spiders.

"I came to tell you that D-D-Darby and I are going to the hospital now, she's h-h-having contractions."

"Oh all right," I answered.

She went on. "We might not be back by morning so you will need to bring the trash cans in from the street after the—um, you know, the g-g-garbage trucks come by at six."

"Oh yes," I said, not sure what else to say. "Bring a nice baby back" might not say what I meant.

They did bring a nice baby back and named him Jeremy.

For a long while the Mothers, as I called Sarah and Darby, almost completely disappeared from my life, so transfixed were they on raising their new baby. Lucky for me as they never did really miss their cat Morgan. Time went fast as Dr. D. had given me a new assignment: plant fruit trees in the long rear yard. The rear yard was like a meadow except for the crabgrass overgrow, so wild a wild goose landed there one year to rest for a while. I dug, using a pitchfork and small sharp shovel to drive through the dense clay. Tore the crabgrass loose again and again until it fell back in discouragement. Lowered those young trees into the holes prepared with compost, water and mulch. Huge reward when the sapling trees quickly took root, made new leaves and smiled at me. No, they did!

Six months went by, a year, then more months. One morning I heard Sarah and Darby talking about wanting the bio-dad to become a real father, a companion father for Jeremy, when I went in their kitchen with a string of onions to trade for some eggshells to feed my worms. There were twelve half-shells right there on the counter, as though earlier they had made an omelet for themselves and a visitor.

"Worms eat egg-eggshells"? Sarah was covering her mouth, laughing. "How do they do that when they don't have teeth?"

I appreciated that she was attempting to relate to me. Resisted snapping my fingers to fix her attention. Looking at the wall to the right side of her face I said, "The eggshells *are* their teeth. They have gizzards, like chickens, and need some grit to chew stuff with."

"Oh!" Sarah now fell all over herself to praise me for being so much smarter (for a minute) than her, and kept moving her head around trying to meet my eyes. I quick grabbed the shells with both hands and ran out the back door. Sometimes living with them is like being in a theater piece. And Sarah had once been a play director, so maybe that explains it.

But before all that happened I heard Dr. Darby say, "He needs a real father, a caretaking father, not just a bio-dad. So let's try and see what happens, shall we?"

Sarah sounded tense when she answered, "Hmmmm . . . maybe. Of course I agree a father figure could be good for him. But I-I-I want to— um, you know—t-t-take it slow at first."

Adopting someone into the family can be tricky, though it didn't seem difficult for the cat family. The Ladies, as I called the mother-daughter pair of them, decided who belonged in the family and who did not. That included me.

One night I got up without turning on any lights to go to the bathroom and as I came out of that room I had the odd sensation of being bumped in the knee. Then again. Then again. Though I could barely see, I soon recognized that the bumper was Morgan. That tiny black cat was literally throwing herself at my legs, hitting her head and shoulders against me. Sleepily, I tried to go around her, and the bumping increased. I stopped. I decided not to negate her actions but to float along with them and see what was happening. Following the directions given by her bumping, I soon found myself across the dining room headed for the kitchen. She wants a midnight snack, I thought, somewhat annoyed. But she blocked my way to that room, switched legs, and bumped more emphatically.

"In here?" I said, unable to imagine why she wanted me to go into the little room, an extra tiny bedroom that was filled—you're not surprised—with seedlings planted in egg cartons. Indulge her, I thought. Be scientific. I turned on the light. Looking me in the face, she trotted to the closet, and when I followed, found Morgan's second litter, black and brown, squirmy, cute as baby eggplants. Felt quite proud to have been invited to attend the grand event. Felt quite thick-headed to have assumed that Morgan was interested only in food. Thus was I invited into their family. And I was not the only one.

One day a young white cat about sixteen weeks old, same as Leah-pard, showed up on the sidewalk in front. Leah brought him into the back yard where I was weeding with Morgan, who was chasing dirt clods around helping me out in her own way. The new cat sat nearby while Leah, very excited, raced between him and her mother, as though to say, "Can we keep him, huh, huh, please Mom?" After a few of these displays, Morgan leaned over toward the new friend and licked him on the head. From then on, he was her son. He took this literally. I called him Willie.

As he grew, his long white body was a leviathan among the tiny Burmese and black babes nursing at her row of spigots. She tolerated him pushing the littler ones aside to claim his nipple; tolerated his superhunger in the kitchen when she provided food for all; and even tolerated him pushing her off any chair he wanted for his own, his huge body squeezing her small one out, over my outraged protests.

The night ward nurse on the sixth floor, the only one I liked even a miniscule amount, had a habit of snapping her fingers when she wanted us to pay attention to what she was saying. For some reason, it worked, mostly, unless we were all bombed on thorazine. So I snapped my fingers at Willie when he took the chair away from his mother Morgan, his true mother.

"She's the one who loves you now, who gets food for you and everything," I told him. Snap. But it didn't help. He always got the chair he wanted. And then he went outside to sit at the curb wailing, as though for his original mother to come get him.

What could be more natural than to put a small boulder of lava rock in the fern bed? My friend Hayscoop, who is huge, helped me do this late on a Saturday night when no one would notice us taking it from a nearby park and putting it in Hayscoop's little red wagon. Now I had a great perch under Sarah and Darby's dining room window to hear a lot of their business because the Mothers say it to each other on Sunday mornings when the clinic is closed and again on Wednesday afternoon when Dr. D. stays home. Sarah calls it "processing the week." I know it's going to happen whenever I hear the gurgle of coffee draining from the glass pot into Dr. D.'s coffee cup and the light clink of Sarah's tea cup brushing the saucer or clattering as she is getting more nervous. I don't use saucers myself, and prefer to eat and drink everything from my forest cup that Hayscoop stole one time and gave me. It's made of ceramic, creamy-colored on the inside, then on the outside it's dark green and has a little enamel picture, blue sky with a tiny forest painting, looks like a window to the earth, and under this the words "Washington State Fair" in gold and brown. I like to imagine I could crawl through that window and come out in deep green trees, this takes my breath away. I know it's possible.

I spend a lot of time underneath the other window, the one in Sarah and Dr. D.'s dining room. Taking my time planting onions and carrots, listening to them talk across their table. Yes, that table. So one Sunday I learned a lot about the bio-dad, Vern.

Sarah was saying, "You went to school with him, what is he like? Why is he so distant most of the time and then b-b-blam!—right in your face?"

Darby used her smooth-as-a-cucumber doctor voice, "Vern's relation to his own father is problematic—his father was a professor at a prominent university, a successful, ambitious man, a golden boy, who was afraid his career would be held back if he gave too much attention to his children. Vern is a hungry son. His father loves him but won't let him in, won't be vulnerable to him—this is my concern, that Vern will emulate his own father, that he has the potential to be short-tempered, critical and competitive."

Sarah's voice was bumpier, with rough panels like a stalk of asparagus: "Well, your own background was somewhat similar to Vern's; you had a mother who b-b-by and large uh-uh-abandoned motherhood."

"Yeah, well Vern's mother gave herself permission to be weak and unable to function well. But my own mother could be tough with me, like, making me sit for an hour with a mouthful of Brussels sprouts which I did not want to swallow, but other times so neglecting kitchen duties that I would come home from school, go into the kitchen and peel a stick of butter to eat as a snack, not knowing any better!" Darby chewing a stick of butter with great gusto was so funny I nearly laughed out loud, and slipped on the stone, feeling the pale-yellow lichens grip the stone tight as my toes skidded over them.

Sarah laughed. "Well, at least you had the butter to eat, but that's ghastly—think of your poor young intestines!" Sarah laughed again and bit down on something crunchy. "Makes me want to go cook you something right now."

"Here, have some marmalade. Bitter orange, your fave. Thanks to living with you I am much better taken care of since my butter days—and healed inside too. Vern hasn't had that advantage."

Sarah said, "I noticed he was sharp-tongued with Jeremy over the *Star Wars* toys."

"Vern has envy because Jeremy gets more attention than he does."

Sarah talked around something in her mouth, "You mean like Vern's disdainful tone when he tells me that Jeremy has too many toys, or he thinks the toy is 'too fancy'?"

"Yes, and also it comes out in Vern not wanting Jeremy to be spoiled. He expects Jeremy to be tough, as he had to be tough." She set her coffee pot down with a thump. "I've had to intervene with him twice lately when he's with Jeremy. The last one was I had to get in the middle of a power struggle between Vern and Jeremy over who was to sit in a particular chair. Can you imagine? The baby was just asserting that this was his house and he has the right to sit where he wants, and Vern was doing this competitive thing, as though, no one in the world—not even a child—has the right to tell him where he can and cannot sit."

I slid backwards right off the rock at this point and had to quick slip away before they could look out the window and see me. I had just learned all about Morgan and Willie—why she gave him even the chair she was sitting in, because he was now her child. He was her big dopey son she would do anything for.

They have their own ways, and those are family ways. I had found Morgan's behavior with her family incomprehensible. Thin and smaller than anyone except the children, that little mother cat solicited food from me relentlessly, as her brood grew in number. Seeing how thin she was, and how constantly she entreated me, I assumed she was starving. I would set heaping bowls in front of her, only to watch as members of her family, including the grown ones, rushed past her and devoured everything, while she continued to solicit.

Furious at what I saw as their rude "animal greed," I pushed them aside, scolded and held back their thundering tide so the Great Mama could eat. But she wouldn't eat, and it took me a while to realize that this was her choice. This was her behavior. And this was her power. She, not I, was feeding them, by contracting for lots of goodies from me. I was the warehouse, she was the grocer. I was nature, she was culture. And she always ate last, after everyone else had their fill and had gone away. Thus, did the matriarch grandmother rule her family. Thus, did the caretaker reign supreme.

When I finally understood this about her, I was moved to humility, and bowed three times to her, touching the top of my hair to the floor. Thus did the caretaker reign over me, as well.

Sunday morning again, the Mothers were processing about—who else?—Vern and Jeremy, father and son. And I was up on my rock, learning.

"Why did you choose Vern as the donor?" Sarah sounded irritated.

"Well, for one thing he's smart, and also small, so I knew it would be an easy birth. And also it was for certain warrior characteristics."

Sarah snorted. "He's a skinny vegetarian who mixes music on soundboards for a living! You on the other hand, you ran an AIDS clinic in defiance of a city aw-aw-ordinance. You're the warrior!"

"No, no, I mean that Vern can finish what he starts, he can go all the way with something and achieve a goal. I know, I can do that too. But at the same time he has a delicate aesthetic, which I know you will agree I just don't have."

Sarah sounded worried as she replied, "Vern is just not easy or joyful with Jeremy. He focuses on perils of every environment, health concerns and fears, possible speech defects, and on and on. He even fusses about the compost heap and Clovis living in the cottage!"

"Yes, he is very particular."

"Speaking of that, what about food? He can go all day eating only bagels. He's very thin, and he thinks he is 'too fat'. He is a strict vegetarian."

Darby snorted this time, "Well, not so strict—he eats nothing 'with a face or that ever had a face.'" Then she softened her tone, "Sarah, you darling. We're lucky that because of you, Jeremy loves food. For Vern, food is something to resist through strength of will. Thanks to you, Jeremy is a little boy who loves broccoli and celery."

"You know I think food is love," Sarah said. "I take cooking very seriously, and I take it personally if it's rejected."

"Is that why the tears this morning?"

"Oh I know it's s-s-silly, but Jeremy didn't want any of his oatmeal."

Darby had her most reassuring tone, "Well, for me, I can step outside this feeling state and ask, what is the bigger question, what is the child really asking for?" At the end she raised the volume of her voice so Sarah must have gone into the kitchen as Darby continued, "For myself, I get upset when he throws things at me or makes other physically aggressive gestures. And in those situations, it's you who stands outside, calmly, and can ask, what is the real question here?" She cleared her throat. Sarah's chair squealed as she returned.

Darby resumed in a normal tone, "I want to tell about something that happened one Wednesday afternoon a few weeks ago, while you were out shopping. It's when I said 'no' to Jeremy for the first time. He had scraped my face with his nails. I said 'No,' and then watched him try out the various limits of the no—he touched my face tenderly and I said, okay; then he curled his fingers next to my cheek and I said that's still okay; then he scraped my face again and I said 'No!' So he wasn't afraid of me, he could explore the whole range of the word 'no' and judge for himself what it was made of."

These last words faded in volume and I knew they had left the room. So I left mine, thinking about Dr. Darby's courage not only with the AIDS clinic, but also bringing me home here to live, even knowing that my dad might show up with his black pickup and wreck everything for everyone before I could even warn them.

The cat mothers were warriors too. Once I witnessed what Morgan and Leah did with an interloper who came into the big house kitchen one day when no one else was there, and I had gone in to make them come out before the Mothers came home from work. The poor bumpkin was a sort of shapeless long-haired, bluish-gray and white cat twice their size without much sense who wandered in thinking to claim turf and then ran into the back bedroom in terror when the Ladies gave chase. The mother-daughter team trapped him up on top of the window on the drapes, which collapsed under their combined weight as they climbed up the cloth, knives in hand, to slash him to bits. Their voices swirling around his ears in a hurricane of hate made him fall, the material wrapping him in a protective shroud as he hit the floor rolling over and over. Gleefully screaming, they mounted and rode him around the room like a bronco, shredding him through the cloth while he bucked and shrieked. I intervened, dragging the whole package to the front door and his blessed release.

The Mothers were upset that an intruder cat had pulled down their drapes. I didn't mention he was chased by the Ladies. When Sarah asked me why on earth a strange cat would climb the floor to ceiling drapes in an inner room, let alone leave the fabric with big puncture marks and threads hanging loose—she looked at me with a such a puzzled expression as though I might have changed size and run up there myself to scare him. Sarah did not believe that female cats were capable of what she called "violence."

I already knew their fearlessness as earlier that year, before Leah had her first family, I looked out the front window just in time to witness the two of them as they approached a wandering Doberman pincer, their whining, siren voices threatening to tear her canine face off, and sent her fleeing full speed down the block with them on her heels, literally, since even bounding at a dead run they were only as high as her ankles.

Where did they get this courage in the face of a ferocious dog? Perhaps it's inherited, but also perhaps it runs in family lines and they learn it. One afternoon, I looked down to see Morgan, Leah, and Morgan's five tiny apricot and black kitties in a single file line, going somewhere in a very focused manner. I followed the line down the fence, and around, along the side of the neighbor's fence, and up to a spot near the neighbor's house. This yard was the daily home of a lonely, bored, noisy terrier mix, a cat-killing dog who earlier that year had destroyed a small wandering feline that fell off the fence into his territory.

The dog was now barking ferociously at the little gathered family, sticking his nose through a hole in the boards in this part of his container, enraged that he couldn't reach them. He had a long, bony nose. Morgan stepped up to the fence just beyond his snarling teeth, lifted her right front paw and smacked the top of his nose six or seven times. Then she sat back. Her daughter Leah came forward, and she too flailed at his nose while he yipped and snarled. She sat back. Then one by one every one of their little kittens stepped up and practiced smacking the snarling dog's nose with their tiny paws. I just bent over laughing.

Maybe I needed some claws too. Lately I'd been seeing the black truck, more than once. So, I sharpened the shears that were for trimming, then practiced stabbing the blades deep into the clay ground. Unfortunately Dr. D saw me doing this, and became unusually upset, she who practiced calmness as a way of life. "Clovis," she said sternly, "you have *got* to take your medicine." I tried, really, I did. I took half doses and quarter doses and full doses and no doses. I occupied myself with the garden and the cats, and with learning about Vern's progress as a caretaker dad. I started reading scripture again, thinking it might calm me down.

The cat family too, had incorporated a caretaking dad. And it wasn't Papa Cat, though with Morgan's blessing, he became her daughter's mate too. Chosen not only for his steadfast character; he was also gorgeously muscled and the smallest of the males who came to ask. But he went away soon after the mating.

Leah-pard's first litter was born in the kitchen, in an open box, and so I got to watch. She had delivered the number one baby with some difficulty, and was noticeably panting. Her mother stayed nearby, sphinx posture, eyes closed, not interfering. Then, to my surprise, her stepbrother Willie got into the box and curled his big body around one corner of the box, cradling her. He put one paw on her belly, as though helping with her contractions. He leaned over to lick the newborn, washing the translucent amniotic sac from its mouth and nose to give it air, while Leah rested. The newborn meowed, and Willie answered. He stayed through two more births. His tired sister rested her head against his shoulder for a few moments, and then he stepped out of the box, and left the room. Though not a bio-dad and never would be (Sarah and I had taken him to the vet to get him neutered soon after he arrived) Willie was sure seeming to be a caretaking dad. Just what the human mothers were looking for.

Leah-pard's first-born daughter was a gorgeous swirl of black and orange, rabbit and apricot, very red in contrast to her black grandmother and brown spotted Burmese looking mother. Their faces were narrow, while she had an impish broad face. I decided to keep her, assuming the three would become a triumvirate of fierce Ladies. But they fooled me again. Morgan and Leah continued to be a tight inseparable pair, and when Rossie, as I called the young lady of the third generation, was twelve weeks old, they gave her to someone else to raise.

They gave her to Willie Weeper, her stepuncle. I was already calling him "weeper" because despite the many ministrations of his stepfamily he missed someone or something terribly and spent the better part of his life out on the front sidewalk calling in a high pitch like a monotonous bagpipe note.

I was lucky enough to be present on the afternoon when the Ladies turned Rossie over to Willie. I sat on a chair against the north kitchen wall, quiet as a lizard, observing. Morgan and Leah were lined up on the west side of the kitchen, facing inward, each in sphinx position, and with barely open, slitted eyes. In the center of the room, Rossie, twelve weeks old, small and gregarious, was lying on her back under Uncle Willie's long white body. They were wrestling. She would shriek and wiggle and he would reach down to bite her. But his teeth never touched her skin. On every motion he made to engage with her body, both mothers began a deep-throated, seriously threatening growling that made him halt, raise his chin and roll his green eyes in their direction.

Rossie continued to wiggle, nip and paw him, shrieking continuously in her baby voice, while he clasped her between his paws, his mouth open, lunging and halting, his ears back listening to the instructions of the mothers. This lesson—which astonished me more than I can say—continued through the afternoon, until the grown females seemed assured that he knew how to be intimate with their baby without hurting her.

From then on, Rossie was Willie's responsibility to raise. During this time he was devoted to her, and spent much less time on the front sidewalk wailing. They were two inseparable chums, usually outdoors romping and exploring. Rossie developed some of Willie's tradition, which differed from Morgan's. Morgan was a great mouser, and Leah was too, she did everything her mom did. I never saw either of them stalk a bird, not even in play. But Willie was a bird hunter, and so was Rossie. The day the two of them slaughtered the block's only mockingbird I scolded them all morning, fruitlessly. The two bird bandits were clearly pleased with the pile of feathers to which they had reduced the mockingbird. I was so mad I kicked the fence and nearly broke my big toe.

Willie and Rossie not only hunted differently, they ate differently. Morgan and Leah both ate brewer's yeast, Leah-pard so avidly she would steal a two pound package off the table and break the plastic open for her babies; I would find yellow powder strewn in deep lines across the kitchen floor, and little rabbit-colored babies standing on the package, their whiskers and faces coated with the golden pollen.

Leah also loved cantaloupe, so much so that once, having followed me to the field portion of my garden, she picked one herself. I was raising little French cantaloupes in the cool summers of the coast. About the size of an orange, they were the only melon that would ripen. I had picked two of them. When I looked back, Leah-pard was trotting on the path behind, head lifted high on her slender neck to account for the third cantaloupe, clutched in her teeth. She presented it to her litter, who were romping on the back steps, and I opened it for them, enjoying how they fell on the cantaloupe as though it was an antelope and they a pride of lions.

In contrast to these habits, Willie and Rossie never ate either brewer's yeast or cantaloupe. And unlike the others, Willie made a snuffling, slurpy noise when he ate, which Rossie took up as well, so that I could tell who was eating just by the sounds emanating from the kitchen. When Rossie grew up she frequently sat with her mother and grandmother, and the three of them occasionally took an herb bath. They would gather together in the herb bed, each vigorously chewing leaves of oregano, marjoram, and thyme plants, until a bubbly white froth appeared on the leaves. They applied this to their cheeks, necks and chests, making a lovely perfume and probably flea deterrent. A family bubble bath.

"Are these cats *rabid*?" Sarah's tone of horror jolted me. She had come down the back steps of her house, which overlooked the herb garden I had planted in a hard clay patch last year. I tried to see what she saw: they did all have bubbly white beards. I explained some of what they were doing but she laughed it away. "I doubt *that*," meaning they weren't smart enough to use plants as medicine. "There must be some catnip in there."

"No," I said.

She cleared her throat. "Well, at least it isn't rabies." She shifted her hips uncomfortably as I went silent, my eyes on the house wall behind her. "Well," she finished, and went back upstairs. Through all this the cats continued calmly making froth.

This is how Sarah was with the cat family, always speaking from her fantasies and fears about them. One day the beautiful Marmalade turned her green eyes up to Sarah's face. "Meow," she said very politely. Sarah looked down at her.

"I'm not going to-to-to *feed* you," she scolded.

"Marmalade just said 'hello,'" I explained.

"We can't afford all these cats," Sarah continued as if I hadn't spoken. But I knew that Marmalade was such a good hunter, she never asked for food. She even brought a moth she had caught into my cottage as a present for the baby kittens, setting the insect body down in front of them as they played in the kitchen.

On the occasion of Rossie's coming of age party, a dozen boy suitors showed up, none of them Papa Cat. The Ladies tore madly around the yard, day after day, chasing them off her. Finally Papa Cat arrived, greeted with affection by the Ladies; he promptly fathered Rossie's litter. Hung out with the family for a couple of weeks as they sat, each on a step, eyes closed, sphinx position, dreaming together I guess. Rossie was a grown-up, and Willie Weeper took up patrol again on the front walk, moaning his deep sorrows.

On a Sunday morning I was near the front of the big house when Sarah swept gracefully up the steps with a sack of what I knew were bakery sweet rolls. They never had shared any of these delectables with me, but I loved to smell the doughy fragrance laced with cinnamon, eating them with my nose so to speak. So I hopped up on my stone under the window, inhaling and almost accidentally listening. As usual, Vern was their subject.

"You seem so much easier with him lately," Darby said.

"Well, it's been a little bit of a bumpy road, uh because your relationship with Vern is very different from mine, I, I don't know him as well and—uh—it was—uh—hard for me not to feel resentful of, of, Vern at first, because he was not participating as much as I thought he should— huh! and I didn't have the buffer of being an old close friend of his that you have." Darby made a sound like a kind of moan.

Sarah continued, "But I see now, with your help, that Vern and Jeremy had to work out their own way of being together, and their own relationship, those were the, the people that we were given, eh, y'know, it was up to them to sort things out, and not up to me to say how they should be, and now that I have stopped grousing about it and am, and am, just letting things develop it's became very pleasurable to have Vern around, and, and, uh, I have started liking Vern a lot better. He and Jeremy get on a lot better; I see them forming a relationship more strongly after, now that Jeremy is verbal, because his dad didn't know how to handle an infant, at least it didn't seem like that to me. Of course—huh! I didn't have any experience in that area either but of course, it, it, came, it came a little more naturally to me than I think to him. Uh—I guess I had a little bit of a competitive thing with him but that has completely—eh—diminished. But, uh, I see that Jeremy finds something with his dad that he can only get from him. It's sort of in-in-indefinable. I can't know exactly what it is but I know it's important. The other day," she was laughing, "Jeremy and I were playing a rhyming game and I was very impressed because he just *volunteered that store— he said*, we were talking about going to the store and *he said store rhymes with poor,* and I said yeah, it does, and then *I said it rhymes with door, and floor,* and a bunch of other things, and I said *what rhymes with day, and he said flay!* and oh some other things, I don't know *where he came up with flay,* I don't even think he knows that it's a word—and we were going on and on playing this rhyming game and *he said daddy rhymes with penis!*" She laughed.

"Which about says it, y'know. And whatever it is that males under-stand about each other, around that, they have—"

Sarah broke in, "And I respect it and I like it. I like Vern a lot better now that he has a love in his life, he has a girlfriend now, that has also opened him up enormously, and he's much more warm and giving, and his, his . . ."

"He's always had a problem with his self-image," Dr. D. finished. I could almost see her licking chocolate doughnut frosting off her fingers, meticulously, taking her time one finger after another, not slobbering the way some do. Me, for example. Dr. D. ate quietly, and I would guess held her head down, her bright eyes flicking up to Sarah's face now and then.

Sarah kept on it, "Every time that Jeremy would cry he would take it personally, but he's grown past that and knows better now, and I think he feels better about himself and so I feel better about everything."

From my rock outside I was thinking, if there is one thing I would want to do if I could not be a gardener it would be to work in that bakery where Sarah goes every Sunday morning. Why? Because those little live yeast cells are so appealing, I feel like they are related to me—bubbling and swelling up with good feelings when everything is warm and moist, and then busting down to something hard and gray, then up again. Smelling so great, you always know when their little yeast bodies have been there, floating in your air.

I was preoccupied with this when something Sarah said clicked in my head. I realized she was a different person than she had been. She'd been saying this:

"Um. Well I, I, yeah, I think after a while he could see that Jeremy was likely to cry for us too, and—he saw us dealing with Jeremy's situations with equanimity and it, it, made him realize that kids are kids and they cry and get cranky with all their parents."

"Yes, and that we honor Vern's place in Jeremy's life I think has made him feel much better about himself."

Sarah kept on, "And uh—I'd love to see, I'd love to see them be more together. 'Cause I think that what happened is that, is that, uh, Vern in some sense felt parented too, I think parenting does help the parent, I feel parented in the situation."

"Yeah," Darby agreed, "I understand my own parents much better, and I see a lot about myself in my own development that I couldn't have known in any other way."

Sarah kept on, "Now I think only in terms of encouraging him more, to spend more time with him. Last year I sometimes I would almost fib, to say, 'Well Jeremy really is looking forward to your coming over,' and actually there were times that Jeremy said he didn't like daddy."

"Yeah, I remember. I think that was because Vern was not very forthcoming and not very giving, he was defended, and held back a lot, and Jeremy picked that up right away."

Sarah continued, "And uh, there was a time that Jeremy didn't really want to invest the child effort, y'know this incredible effort that children make, to bond, to relate, they really put themselves out and they, they, try everything, to be sure that they, they, *have* you, and I think there was a time he didn't think daddy was worth all that." She laughed. "'No, I don't like daddy,' he would say, and that was during the time we especially wanted them to have time together because we figured that that would help them sort of meet each other halfway."

"And it did," Darby affirmed.

Sarah continued, "I think the only thing we did in the way of steering how things went w-was to invite him around a lot more, just to be sure that, uh—and I have to say I, I, didn't enjoy Vern's company in those old days, I really didn't, he was very self-centered, he would come plowing into the kitchen and say, 'Oh I've got a terrible cold,' and 'Oh I haven't gotten any sleep,' and 'Oh I'm having problems with my, y'know—*job*,' and he was going to come in and tell us all about his life. But that too has, um, changed a little bit, I think just continued exposure to each other and continued willingness to try and make the situation grow h-has helped all of us."

Darby sounded ready to stop, "Uhuh."

Sarah had one more point, "It really has helped all of us, I mean, I had my narcissistic streak, still do, that sometimes, uh, takes me away from . . . uh, uh, situations or, or, makes me not optimal in it, y'know, so I recognize that, I recognize myself in Vern, and sometimes I, I, would resent that I had no choice but to overcome my narcissism, and, and, do all the stuff that you have to do for a kid, you know, you just have to drop everything, and I wanted him to know some of that too and in a mean kind of way but the funny thing is, the funny thing is that when you make those sacrifices, and they're really rather small in the scheme of things, you feel good."

So there was Sarah comparing herself to Vern. I went away from under the window feeling better about her, as well as being full from the doughnut smells. Yet for some reason in the next few days I kept getting mad at everything. Maybe it was because I was trying to tell them: "And another angel came out of the altar, which had power over fire, and cried a loud cry to him that had a sharp sickle, saying Thrust in thy sharp sickle, and gather the clusters of the vine of the earth, for her grapes are fully ripe." I hand-wrote this on a piece of paper, added "Rev. 14:18" and slid it under their back door. A minute later the door opened and Sarah stood there with the paper in hand, looking distracted. Instead of responding to my message, Sarah asked me why I was rubbing my eye with my knuckles. I did not want to tell her that I was practicing washing my face like a cat. Had licked the knuckle first. Getting ready. So when she suggested "allergies?" I nodded, and afterwards was grumpy at myself, because it was a lie.

One day sitting on the top of the back steps drinking coffee from the beautiful and may I say magical cup Hayscoop had stolen for me, which I don't usually drink, but Sarah had left some in their kitchen so I sneaked it but then I got so mad, I stood up and threw the cup at the sidewalk by the hedge, as hard as I could. The cup hit the cement but instead of a satisfying shatter, it bounced straight up in the air for about twenty feet, and then vanished. I mean vanished. I looked everywhere, all through the hedge, the neighbor's yard, the garden on that side. Nothing.

So I'm thinking did it go into a different dimension? Were things better there, as cup lives go? Did it, at the top of its arc, just step off the material planet, without so much as a crack or flash? And given that it bounced straight up without shattering, had the molecules that named it "ceramic" fused into something else before it even landed? Were the molecules fired by the rage that flamed in my launching hand, and did the cup change into something that could get into the mind of everything?

The behavior of Morgan and Leah on the afternoon they instructed Willie how to be gentle with their daughter left me with other questions: how did they decide, together, to turn Rossie's education over to Willie Weeper? By what means did they communicate this possibility, desire, and decision, to each other? How did they know what method would work to effect the transfer? How did he know to listen to them? It's like they too had a window to a forest where they all lived in their minds together. I wanted to live there with them!

Everything was going well with the cat family, and for Sarah and Darby's family, they were getting closer. Everything was going pretty well for me too, so I knew it was time to worry. Garden was flourishing. My nine corn plants had grown tall—the red kind, chattering together in a double row. Corn is talkative, always rustling. The long green tomato horn worms that I borrowed from a garden the next street over, had turned into enormous charcoal gray moths the size of bats. I went out at night to see them hanging on the side of the fence, so graceful, waiting for their next step.

Last night I dreamed the end of everything. My dad's black truck had arrived, parked in front of Dr. Darby's house. All kinds of people were lined up down the block, and I lined up too, so did Sarah, Dr. D. came, carrying Jeremy, who was looking backward over her shoulder.

My hands were full of plants and lumps of earth, and as I got closer to the open door of the truck red worms wriggled out of my hands and fled; strawberries were running down my arms like little red mice and getting away. But I wasn't, so I began to shake, felt sure I was about to get in. Knew this was a very bad idea. Hung in that moment of knowing. Then it happened, I stepped into the truck. The whole inside was liquid with flames. Beautiful yellow, red, and blue fire, just melting everything. Metal and plastic parts of the truck dissolving. I took a breath. Even knowing better I had climbed into that truck. Snap!

THREE

More Accounts
Three Forms of Consciousness

Mind inhabits us and we inhabit mind. My own experiences, enhanced by the suppositions of scientists, psychologists, and philosophers, tell me that there are three levels of my conscious being: first is the unconscious as a matrix of tiny beings continually interacting with my cells; second is the everyday awareness fed through my senses (touch, sight, sound, smell, taste); and thirdly are those occasional breathtaking moments of radiant intelligence or feeling from unknown sources outside myself. The following three pieces are full of anecdotes that are completely true to the best of my ability, and address aspects of these three states of consciousness.

Elementals

The huge Monterey pine in our yard grew up fifty years ago from a potted plant giveaway by a local bank. The generously spreading tree is well-used by local wildlife, including a family of small black squirrels. The young ones use it as part of their speedway on those days in spring when the family practices agility, and the youngsters leap from the tree to the roof, then leap again to spiral down the forty foot redwood on the other side of the house, along the fence, then spring across to the apple tree then to the garage, fence again and up the pine tree, round and round and round all morning long, chasing each other as fast as they can go. The mother squirrel the last few years has been a gardener as well, carefully harvesting about a third of my sprouting potatoes and onions and taking them home for breakfast. Occasionally replanting the potatoes in the other end of the bed. I got to know her pretty well, her eyes bright on mine as she swept across the yard mouth swollen with her forage. I would laugh; I like potatoes and onions for breakfast too, and don't need all that grow in my garden.

Then odd bits began showing up in the little yard. A number of whole walnuts still in their hulls from the tree across the street, unaccountably showing up on my porch. Then, another year, food the dog gnawed on that could only have come from outside the yard: chicken bones, an avocado, more walnuts, and—left to rot—a grapefruit. A mysterious gift-giver was afoot, leaving things for the dog's interest. And I had seen a squirrel run across the fence line, head high with a grapefruit in mouth. One day, with a friend, I was walking our dog on his leash, around the block. After the first turn a black squirrel raced up a tree in front of us, and as we passed, dropped a bone—I swear!—on the sidewalk. Unmistakably given to us.

Last year the mama ripped the rotting seat cover from an abandoned chair in the yard, and took small bits of green plastic stuffing for her nest, leaving a trail of green fluff going up into the redwood's thick green limbs. I imagined the squirlets cuddled into the soft padding of their bed, waiting for mom and onion-smelling milk.

Then tragedy. I went out one morning as heavy wind and rainstorm tossed the tree limbs, and mama squirrel lay underneath the redwood tree on the brick paving, her back broken. Rain poured down on her. Above, the many long leaves of the redwood thrashed and heaved.

Wanting her to be dry at least, I placed the tall domed lid of the barbecue protectively over her, then went inside to get out of the fierce rain myself. Evidently either the wind or a predatory raccoon or skunk family had attacked her house and she had fallen. I came outside to look at her again about thirty minutes later. She half rose and turned her head to meet my eyes, holding the intent gaze for a very long time. I felt she was communicating, yet I could not read the message. She lowered her head, and died. No psychic connection enabled me to read her final expression, only that it was long and deep. With my five senses alone, I could not read her mind, though I grieved for her and her abandoned young for weeks afterward, especially when finding the bits of green plastic blowing around the yard. I also wanted to know what her look meant, and I never shall. Some messages don't get delivered; I can't open the psychic channel at will.

But some messages *do* get delivered. I study my dog's body language to understand him better, though I haven't gotten dreams or other psychic information from him. I was talking to him about this recently. A couple nights later I awoke in the deep of night because a dark shape, like a palm, was passing in front of my eyes, not like a shadow, like something inside my head. Startled, I opened my eyes and there was the dog right in my face, his bright eyes shining at me.

"What is it!" I shouted, startled, and his face had a smiley look as he turned and trotted back to his own bed. So, okay, even without training I can sometimes ask for a connection and have it happen. So far, my examples have been about creature-to-creature psychic connections and attempted connections. I could not reach the squirrel's mind, but my dog friend reached mine. Transmission and reception both need to be functional.

Now I am curious about our other less accessible companions on earth—the elements, especially stone, and fearsome fire. How could we know if they interact with us or have anything resembling our sense of consciousness? I could not "read" the squirrel's gaze. How much more difficult to understand stone or fire?

Yet like lots of people I become very attracted to stones and bring them home, ordinary stones. Little stacks of two to four typically occupy one the corner of the living room. By "little" I mean quarter pound, hand-sized or smaller. The most handsome is a green and brown stone with smooth grooves along its sides that fit my fingers perfectly, and a blunt end like a hammer. Holding it I can imagine a human having made it a few thousand years ago, or not; a river could have made it too, for all I know. This stone is so companionable I keep it on a table near my bed and look at it often. When in the past I have moved and lost it temporarily to the mysteries of unpacked boxes, I miss it. To those close to me I say, "Remember that green stone? I wonder where it is."

I wonder if it misses me.

I remember certain stones with the same sense of "knowing someone special" that I have for longtime friends, memorable people I have met, animal companions who have passed on, trees I have engaged in passionate monologue. And—certain stones. Not so much precious stones, jewelry stones or crystals. I love best ordinary-looking river stones, beach stones, mountain rocks, and rock formations I have spent time near. In my house and sometimes in my car, small stones that weigh a pound or less have been tucked into the corners. What are they doing there? For protection, something to be thrown at an intruder? No, this has never occurred to me. The stones are there because they keep me company. How they do this I have no idea.

My own Scandinavian ancestors evidently had no problem with this question, naming and interacting with spirits inhabiting rocks and water. One name for these is vaettur (plural), specifically landvaettur, those spirits living in stones, and vatnavaettur for those in water, especially waterfalls. The Vanir were an ancient matriarchal people whose goddess Freyja was approached through magical practices involving land spirits. Landisir were protective female ancestral spirits who live in rocks. Disir are one's maternal ancestors, while one's paternal ancestors are Alfar, Elves.

Even eighteenth-century preindustrial Sweden was a land crowded with spirits, or vaettur. Land wights was another North European term for spirits who live in stones and waterfalls. If needing to move a stone, a practice was to bring the stone some food, eat some, then leave some.

Honoring includes warning them when doing anything startling like throwing boiling water or urine on the land. The spirits inhabit all aspects of landscape, including caves and trees. They can take the shape of troll-like animals and they can possess human beings. My ancestors in all probability made offerings to the spirits of the family, the disir, with offerings called disablöt, of fruits, ales, or pigs, usually at the beginning of winter. The spirits, associated with Freyja, bring bounty and bless newborns. The wights can tell about your future.

My American-assimilated parents did not directly speak about any latter-day interactions with land spirits. However, I would guess it was my father who taught me to leave a little bite on my plate after eating, "for the fairies."

While my Scandinavian ancestors clearly understood that stones serve as locations for spirit energies, they were hardly the only peoples to perceive this, as the oldest surviving goddess installations are stones, often associated with the Earth goddess Ma. She was the Giantess (mountain) of north Europe, the rib-shaped dolmens from the Pyrenees to the Korean peninsula, the stone pelvic laps on which people sat to ask for a child or love or health, the flat plain stone recipients of food and prayer of parts of India and South Asia, the carved goddess and snake stones of Greece, the stones that bleed in Indian as well as North and South American community practices; the stones that bring rain in San Diego County, the stones activated by blood offerings in remote villages out of sight of disapproving eyes. Archaeologist Marija Gimbutas found thousands of small stone figures she identified as goddess ikons in sites of Old Europe. And a common practice today is the wearing of polished, semiprecious stones to either conduct or deflect body energies and are used as amulets wherever the "Evil Eye" continues to be a known hazard.

Stones of Mother Earth

The most impressive stones I have ever met are enormous boulders that have heaved up out of the soil on a mountain in San Diego County, called by indigenous peoples who spent their summers there (before they were forcibly displaced) gathering and processing acorns a century and a half ago: "Mountain of Moonlit Rocks." Made of intrusive igneous rock similar to granite except coarser and struck through with gleaming bits of quartz and mica, black ore in spots, and occasional runny-looking red iron extrusions.

The boulders split easily and often in intense weather, and their surfaces easily read as enormous faces, creatures, profiles of bodies, and, especially, vulvas. San Diego county terrain is full of archeological sites known as "vulva stones" worked by human hand into unmistakably female sacred sites. Friends of mine, Betty de Shong Meador and Mel Kettner who own and live on a ranch in the foothills of this mountain, have found such a site on their land.

Mel was led to the heavily overgrown site through his use of a dowsing stick. Mel's method of dowsing was traditional European, holding the ends of a forked tree limb and walking while asking a question. The wand makes a sudden downward or upward twisting motion when the answer is underfoot or nearby. Looking for signs of earlier habitation, Mel first found a waist-high stone wall, and some rectangular house walls; then following out from a line of wall, he continued to use his dowsing implement which led him to a spot overgrown with thick plants. The wand told him something was under the massive foliage, and ducking under limbs, pushing away the overgrowth, he found a goddess installation from long ago. She is a big rounded gray stone with white splotches and a split on top that forms a very realistic round pelvis and vulva shape, no trunk, legs, or head. She is literally a vulva of the earth, about waist-high, very accessible—you can sit on one side of her. Extrusions of red shading into pink mark the slit of the internal lips of her vulva, and there is suggestion of a clitoris. As though in whimsy, a bit of mossy lichen grows at the top of the slit, like green pubic hair.

A little research and Mel's wife Betty discovered that San Diego has many such installations, understood as having been created by ancestors of Tipai or Ipai peoples, who as I said spent summer seasons living in the inland mountains near oak groves, grinding acorn meal near streams and hunting small game. An adjoining ranch, now a nature preserve, also has a standing rock formation goddess or mother earth figure; red-stained lichens grow in a circular flower shape around her clitoral head; the labial lips of her vulva contain two oval human-made carvings that are familiar to archeologists over a broad range of the earth's surface. These carvings are associated with the vulva shape, perhaps carved as part of puberty rites or by women requesting a wanted pregnancy, or a change in weather. Perhaps each supplicant dug a bit of grainy stone and ate it as part of a pregnancy prayer, with earth mother as one of the parents of any child that was then conceived. In San Diego County, the carvings are also believed to have been used to conjure rain or snow. According to archaeologists, shamans of San Diego's indigenous communities scraped a bit of stone with a fingernail and ingested it as part of rain-making.

Stone connections are part of our scientific/spiritual ancestral past, and of people intersecting and communicating with stones as sentient beings, practiced on every continent, part of a very old human idea of Earth as Ma, as Mother, whose bones are made of stone.

Touched by Spirit

Of course, on the face of it, it's by definition not possible to "touch spirit" if spirit is "unembodied presence." Yet, altered states have a distinctive "feel" and exercises to perceive someone's energy from across the room produce that feeling as well. Once when a friend died, I was sleeping in the next room and woke at a little after 5:00 a.m., the time he died, to a sense of my aura field having been "brushed." I certainly felt touched. And the particular heart opening that is ecstatic and nearly painful definitely feels like a touch, a beam, a wave, from outside.

But I can't say that extraordinary experiences with the elements translate as "touch" in such ways. The idea, perhaps, is that a landvaettir is a spirit presence that *inhabits* rather than *is* the stone. The stone is to be given food (ordinary human food). This seems congruent with practices in Asia in which feeding stones is for the purpose of creating a welcoming place, or seat, for the desired deity or spirit to stay while it (or He/She) is addressed, or to keep it calm and pleased. Offerings are of all kinds, foods, song, dance, poems, drawings, water, fire and a variety of powders. Even though long secular in practices, some European communities spill a bit of beer or wine on the ground prior to drinking, acknowledgement of Earth Ma, I like to suppose. At the very least such practices keep us a little more humble and connected to the sources of our lives.

An example of stone that emanates the love that is poured toward it is the Naga snake statues in goddess temples in India. These carved stone icons originated as guardians of wild groves preserved at the back of people's yards and gardens; many of the little statues, carvings of upright cobras, have been taken to the temples for safekeeping as contemporary life robs everyone of the time and attention that once could be devoted to keeping the Naga spirits lively. These statues, mostly about a foot and a half high, are gray stones carved with dramatic upright hoods characteristic of cobras. The hoods and tops of their heads are coated with orange turmeric powder, the offering given to them by the people who love them. This love stays with the statues, and is discernible, palpable in my heart when I am standing in front of them. To me it feels like a warmly spreading benevolent and joyful feeling of good will and peace. It is powerful, distinctive, and real.

Real cobra snakes inhabit the countryside, villages, and suburbs; they are never to be killed or tormented as extreme harm is believed to follow any such action. Members of one of Kerala's communities play on a single string instrument, the Tumbi, a haunting song in the temples to honor the Nagas. Members of this group hold that snakes are the animation, the life fire, of the earth.

In the modern world, do stones interact with us? We interact with versions of them all day, in our buildings, cars, roads, machines, cooking utensils and so on. Everything metal in our lives comes from stone. Stones are mineral, so if we wear jewelry, we are draped with stones. But I've never noticed anything I would call communication *with* a stone or any metal extracted from stone. A friend, however, had a distinctly communicative experience with a metal bowl.

Susan Abbott and Dee Dee Bloom lived together in a loving relationship for forty-four years, until Dee Dee grew gravely ill and passed away. Dee Dee had owned a Tibetan singing bowl that she bought in the little coastal town of Inverness, California. The bowl was crafted by Zen monks in South Korea, from a quartz-gold alloy, which gave it a very clear tone. Gold is conductive of electromagnetic waves and quartz would magnify this effect. Susan gave permission for me to quote the following account:

"Dee Dee did not use the bowl every day. Much of the time it was in its storage box and brought out to play mostly for healing circles or meditation. My sister took it out to play for Dee Dee during her final days and I have since just kept it on top of the chest where her medicines were kept. I played it on and off in the vigil of the night of her passing which was this past Sunday night to Monday morning. This morning around eight thirty, the third day since her passing, I was in the dining room having my morning cuppa and I heard this low deep sound seemed to be coming from the bedroom and I went to investigate and it was the bowl. It lasted about a minute. . . . I never heard it spontaneously erupt before. It was one of Dee Dee's few treasures in the world. She didn't leave much stuff behind but she wanted my sister to have that bowl. Meanwhile she used it to say hello today in a deep yet playful tone of soothing comfort. I felt the resonance especially in my heart."

As I understand this, the stone elements in the finely made bowl conveyed a message "from the other side," from someone who had become an ancestor, living in the nonmaterial, or should we say *less* material, part of the universe, and as is so often the case, the message was one of love.

Fire and Stone

While I love to have small amounts of fire close by, I'm never temped to get in it, nor to walk across hot coals. The element of fire, though a chemical process, also emits waves and can be placed on the spectrum of electromagnetism, somewhere between slow radio waves and ultrafast X-rays and gamma rays. Fire emits all kinds of waves; I don't see why it isn't capable of sending messages. By "fire" I mean something manageable to scale, like a candle or small lamp. When I send focus and love to my spouse by staring at a candle, wherever she may be, she reports feeling this.

Billions of human beings, myself included, will set a little fire in order to send a message. We light a small oil lamp or candle to encourage the sick, ease the process of dying, and to send love to our dearly departed; we carry them in processions of silent protest; we wear them on our heads to mark winter solstice and call back the sun; we set them on our tables and line up votaries in front of our altars; we set candles afloat in the sea or around the roofs of our houses at holidays. Often, I stare into the tiny flame of a candle while thinking of another person, sending hope or love. I think of this as a sacred practice, and of myself as a tiny bit of a fire priestess, doing this for people I care about.

But a real fire priestess has a great deal more power than this. My friend and early mentor Mac had his life saved by such a priestess. Robert E. MacDaniel was born in Mississippi, in a rural location far from towns and a doctor. When he was less than six months old, he rolled into an open fire, and the top of his head burned. No matter what his mother did for the wound, it didn't heal; the crust became a suppurating cap over his head. Over the next couple of weeks, the baby lost weight and began to die. In a last effort the white Christian family called in a "fire-talker," a healer from the nearby African American community. Mac said she took him into a room and closed the door for thirty minutes while she "talked to the fire." His mother told him that he began to heal immediately and was soon completely well.

In his late teens MacDaniel hitchhiked out of Mississippi, attended college, became a nuclear physicist, and moved to New Mexico, where I fortunately met him when I was seventeen. Mac, who had such severe rheumatoid arthritis that he weighed only about eighty pounds and was often bed-ridden, sported a beautiful thick beard, and became an invaluable mentor for young women in the area. He encouraged our intelligence, education, and ambition, and though he was thirty when I knew him, with his red beard and sense of humor, he was like a father or wise older brother figure standing at the gates of adulthood, urging us to leap into the biggest possible ponds we could find. His encouragement was a huge gift to a great many of us; without that fire-talker, he would never have been a part of our lives.

In much more dramatic fashion, peoples especially with an Earth goddess practice use fire to display "faith." By this I think what is meant is capacity to raise one's own mental center, or let go of enough ego-identification to raise your vibratory rate to more closely cohere with spirit. A test of this I have witnessed and read about in India includes walking barefoot on hot coals without burns, something done in contemporary Wiccan and New Age practices. More demanding in rural India practice was to carry another adult on one's shoulders while crossing a hot coal bed the width of a small river. Other fire tests (from a hundred years ago or more) included plunging one's hand into boiling porridge, or even pouring the pot of porridge over one's head (do not try this at home!). Well I can hardly imagine being in that much of a trance, though I do on occasion perceive my center of attention, of consciousness, as a few feet above my head.

My experience with fire ritual in Kerala, South India required me to be grounded and present, though I did experience merging my identification with a lamp. During my four visits to this complex and interesting culture, my American colleague who is, among other things, my India mentor, Dianne E. Jenett, and I attended and filmed, a variety of dramatic rituals. One temple ritual that we participated in views a simple brass lamp as the deity.

While I was used to candles as the light source in ritual, in Kerala, and throughout India, the light source in ritual is the more dramatic blaze of the oil-burning brass lamp. Generally cast as a bowl shape that may or may not include a stem, the bowl is filled with sesame oil (*gingelly*), whose rich natural color against the bronze metal of the lamp gleams all the more red. Some lamps have a *yoni* appearance, such as one I brought home that has a lip with a slot for the wick in a most deliciously evocative clitoral-like shape. This one also has a bronze back piece featuring a cast of goddess Lakshmi—a *dipalakshmi*; the rim of the bowl has two cast birds—roosters. Other typical Kerala lamps include a *lingam* shape rising from the bowl; the goddess is not singular, she has many aspects and lots of sister and companion deities, including Shiva.

Wicks of white twisted cotton lie in the bowl; saturated in *gingelly*, their tips are turned up at the rim to keep the small flame burning bright and free. Typically two wicks are joined together, and two, three, or four little flames set evenly apart to burn at the edges of the glowing bowl, reflected in the oil as well as the bronze. The beauty, symmetry, and energy of blazing lamps in Hindu ritual help make the proceedings particularly dynamic.

One woman described to me a meaning of the act of circling the fire, as "symbolic of your life, the course of your living," with the god at the center of the flame. "The fire is about burning without leaving a residue," she said. Whatever we do, it should then immediately fall away without a trace, "This is the ideal, the most ideal realization of the goddess practices."

She also told me that in temple practice, "*Arati* is a big handheld round lamp lit by the head priest at the end of a *puja*; he circles it in front of the goddess. The priests put part of the sanctified fire on a plate and pass it around to devotees, who reach into it and put it on themselves." I experienced this later, reaching into the flame in the temples, a particularly exciting part of the proceedings when the priests bring dramatic plates of flame into the crowd. Stretching out your arm along with dozens of others, you reach into the flame and then rub your palm on your face. This has a cleansing, brightening effect.

In some Indian communities the lamp is understood mythically as a version of, and as related to, the sun, whether gendered as god or goddess. The pious woman's task of lighting the lamp at dusk is sometimes described as "preserving the sun's light until morning," or another way of saying this is just that it's a connection of spirit in nature, and a dedicated tribute to the life-giving force of light.

In public rituals the lamp may become infused with the spirit of the goddess, as for example, at the dramatic enactment called Mudiyettu, she is Kali in the form of a lamp, and offered prayers and flowers. In pan-Indian religion, goddess Lakshmi can take the form of a lamp. Women of a Tiyya community in north Malabar, at Cannanore—who are not Muslim—told a story about two sister goddesses, one of whom went to live in the local mosque in the form of a lamp, so they could never be permanently separated, as the Hindu sister could visit her sister in her lamp form once a year.

My own experience of knowing the goddess as a lamp became very deeply personal:

Attukal temple was the site of Aswarya Pula, a women's ritual in which my travel companion Dianne E. Jenett participated in February of 1997 and both of us participated in March of the next year. In this afternoon ritual offering to a goddess named "Bhagavathi," or more affectionately and generically, "Devi," we sat shoulder-to-shoulder with lines of women facing each other on an open pavilion at the east side of the temple. A Nayar woman who had graciously met with us previously was the leader of the *bajans*. These songs, which we sang in call and response form, all centered on praising Devi and saying her names. The ritual consisted of numerous exact small motions directed to a lamp. Each participant was sitting in front of a small lamp, about six inches high, a base and stem with a round trough for the oil, out of which emerged the lingam shape pointing upward. We were also given packets, containing two wicks, a plantain leaf to serve as a platter holding a number of small items wrapped in newspaper—flowers, incense, sandalwood paste, and red *cum-cum* powder and so on—the standard items used in *pujas*. In effect, each of us was her own priestess performing a *puja* identical to those of all the other women.

My journal notes on Full Moon ritual at Attukal Temple:

"Sunday (March 23, 1997). I was sick from bus exhaust and the mothballs used to control insects in the hotel—could not eat. The heat debilitating. Dianne went to the men's Ayappa street fair, and ate the feast (everyone says her ability to eat *paisam*—the sweet runny rice pudding—with her hand means she lived a former life as a Hindu). At this feast the food was served on highly revered green banana leaf plates, set directly on the street. When she returned she didn't want me to be sick so she drew me a beautiful *kolam* (ground drawing) with her chalks and I rallied enough to go with her to attend the Full Moon women's ritual at Attukal Temple.

"We took off our sandals and entered the temple yard, going to an outdoor pavilion to the left of the temple entrance. The pavilion was packed with women seated in long rows back to back with each other. This rite is growing—from two hundred attendees two months ago to three hundred and fifty and more.

"I didn't think I could possibly sit cross-legged for two hours but I actually did as well as some of the other first-timers. We each had a flat green banana leaf and a small bronze lamp directly in front of us, and we were facing women in another row who also had lamps. Moving quickly, we had to unwrap six or eight little packages of various offering substances, red powder (*cum-cum*), sandalwood paste, flower petals and so on. We had to place everything correctly on our banana leaves, light two wicks in our lamp and mark the four sides of the lamp with three pastes in exact order, hold flower petals between thumb and forefinger and pile them a certain way, hold red powder (*cum-cum*) and pile it a certain way, all while holding positions, using only certain fingers, moving rapidly, chanting verses, and tending the fires—we walked down the rows beside the narrow mats without setting fire to ourselves, touched foreheads to the floor without knocking anything about—."

I see from these notes how concerned I was with my stamina, my ability to contain my body and not be clumsy in these close quarters. We sat cross-legged, knee-to-knee on the floor—not my most favored posture. The lamp was central to our attention and required much care. The little cotton wicks, one on each side of the round central trough, one of mine consistently drooped over the edge and went out, while the other slid far down and drowned in the lake of oil. To stay lit the wicks had to stay fixed, just so. We each—three hundred fifty women—touched our faces and hearts with the flower petals, in time with each other and with the rhythm of the songs. We piled the delicate petals a few at a time at the bases of the lamps in front of us.

As I struggled with the rapid, delicate, and unaccustomed gestures, after a while finding the rhythm and falling into a trance, I began to see the little lamp turning into a person, with her skirt of red and white petals, (as I gradually heaped them up), and her abdominal bowl of glowing red oil, her twin *shakti* flames alive with interactive animation, the top of the lamp her brass *lingam* of inclusiveness and bi-gendering. The interaction of the rite included that the lamp required each woman's intermittent care with the level of oil—we passed around a large vessel of oil and helped each other feed the small individual lamps—and the burning wicks, which needed frequent rearrangement with one's fingertips. The interaction with the flame was very personal, and of course a bit uncomfortable, riding as it did between the bowl running out of oil, or the tender flames drowning, or alternatively, burning my own tender fingers.

Continuing the songs and repeated gestures, my vision changed from seeing Devi in the shape of the lamp to seeing and feeling her in myself as well, especially because the ritual required touching a few flower petals to my body, my heart and throat, before placing them in her ever-growing "skirt." I began to directly connect to the lamp as myself, and her; my body as a lamp, and her.

The light of the lamp reflected and described the spirit of the deity in me, and soon also in my view of the women sitting opposite and beside me. I began to feel compassion for them, coming from work—all women work hard in this current economy—to do this ritual together. I saw—in heightened sensibility—the incredible beauty of their dress and the serious intent of their demeanor. Synchronizing my body and breath with the rhythms of the songs and all our intricate motions involving such simple yet timeless paraphernalia: hand to heart to lamp with flower petals, sandal paste, red powder, I was moved to mutual compassion by the efforts we all made to make our motions timely and graceful. I saw these as the motions of our lives.

I also saw that a few of the other women were as new at doing this rite as I, and they too struggled not to lose attentiveness to the flame at the wick's tip, and to the exacting order of the ingredients. One of them too had difficulty with the cross-legged posture and another had sweat on her upper lip keeping up the pace of intricate motions. This observation calmed me. I stopped judging myself so harshly as an "outsider." I had empathy for them and thus for myself as a beginner. When my back muscles collapsed in pain under the unaccustomed posture almost immediately the woman behind me shifted and leaned her own back against mine, supporting me. How did she know I needed that? Helpless, I was held, an experience repeated often during my stay in Kerala.

The last portion of the Full Moon rite we all stood and walked the course of our narrow lines, following the rectangular path like a gauntlet-labyrinth between the rows of plantain leaves and burning lamps, still singing, stepping with our heads up, trusting our lightweight flowing clothing would not drift into the fires. Now, instead of tending the vulnerable wicks of the lamp, we moved in appreciation of her terrible flaming power. Her capacity to reach out and burn us, balanced by the steadiness we needed to walk her narrow way, and look good while we did so.

Once returned to our own places we sat for the last *bajan* and the cleanup of our paraphernalia. My journal notes record that we kneeled and touched our foreheads to the floor, though I now have no memory of this and cannot imagine how I did it in such close quarters.

I was proud of my accomplishment of this rite—I who feel so frequently like an outsider even under my own roof, to feel so much that night like an "insider," and a woman among women in a society and an era in which women's work is exacting, rigorous, and artful. To experience the lamp as an extension of myself, and me as an extension of the lamp, circling, through the course of a life. Trying to contain all that power while at the same time appreciating the small motions that make a life functional.

Messages of Fire

Dianne E. Jenett and I came back from our India trip so full of *shakti* energy from attending goddess rituals that the computer and editing equipment we needed to show our research simply wouldn't work. Everything stalled. Dianne slathered turmeric and sandalwood paste on the machinery to help it cool down, from a bio-energetic point of view. Then when we had film enough to show, we were putting out so much bodily heat that when we presented our report to other students in our program, they scooted twelve feet away from us, "Because you are so hot," they said. They didn't mean sexy. They meant we were pouring out extra energy in the form of waves of heat.

I've always run high energy that is easily knocked off balance, with a startle reflex that sends kitchen utensils flying here and there. I also have an erratic relationship with electronic keyboards. Music excites me, and when I got a twenty-four key Korg electronic synthesizer, it soon had a nervous breakdown under the excitement of my fingers; chords sounded like crushed tin cans, individual keys made different yowling noises or gasps. Interesting, but nothing on a scale. More like fighting cats shrieking. The sales guy said their equipment never had such a breakdown, and gave me a replacement, which lasted about a week before it too, melted into incoherence. I traded up for a fifty-one key instrument; this more substantial one held up better for a few weeks, but after a while it too began to change from note to metallic scream and I recognized the pre-psychotic break. I asked my friend Ruth Rhoten, the silversmith, for help. She makes tools that can redistribute subtle body energy, as it's called. (Mine wasn't subtle but who's parsing). She created a silver and lapis lazuli, shield-shaped implement, about two inches wide and long, flat, that attached to the top of my keyboard with Velcro. If I touched the fingertips of my left hand to it when the excitement built and the notes began to shatter and whine, everything stabilized. I used that keyboard for years.

One more example of light and bodies: my spouse, Kris Brandenburger, and I in the 1980s practiced sending images back and forth during prolonged sex. One afternoon, my eyes picked up a tiny, miniscule beam of light from the sun, a mote in the shape of a cell, caught at the edge of the windowsill near our bed. I focused on this image and afterward asked what she had seen. She described a shape of light coming into view within her mind, as her eyes had been closed (do try this at home, especially if you are over forty and more grounded!).

Our bodies contain minerals, and it is minerals in water that cause it to conduct electricity; this must be true in our bodies as well. Because of my self-observed experiences, I have to believe that our energies can, in certain circumstances, impact material reality. And that this is just part of organic life, no reason to demonize any of it, any more than we demonize electric lights, laser surgery, iPhones, and Wi-Fi. It's all magic, and all with a physical basis.

And a psychic connection can also be present. Kris, who spent many years with her own electrical repair shop, specialized in working with the electrical systems of vintage racing cars and other classic autos. Dealers sent her work even from overseas, and she solved seemingly impossible wiring problems; for example, a coachbuilt car whose wires had all burned, and no diagram existed. She seemed to have a psychic connection with her work, often intuiting solutions others could not find. Once, after months of trying to solve a wiring problem that had occurred in the factory, she dreamed that the solution was in an inaccessible and not-obvious place; a rear door pillar.

The mineral world interacts with us, and conducts our fire, our intentional waves. Thin metal wires transmit our pictures, all around the world. The air carries our voices on radio waves of electromagnetic radiation, waves with oscillations of hills and valleys, whose unique frequency is the number of waves per second. The stone world is either conductive or insulating; the minerals conduct electromagnetic energy or they put a wall around it. In Gay slang terms, they are butch or femme, ground or vivacity. And fire is always vivacity.

When I feel unsure, shaky or hyperexcited, holding a small stone calms me down. Whenever I feel a need to send love or some other message all day long to someone, a little flame is my go-to messenger. I like to imagine that the flame connects in some way to a ray of some kind and transmits my message, even across hundreds of miles. In my experience ordinary stones and small flames can change my feeling states, as well as transmit energies and messages. And I wonder, were my ancestors feeding the stones, as such, or rather the spirits associated with stones, the landvaettur?

Rupert Sheldrake, in *Science and Spiritual Practices*, moves beyond the worn-out depiction of a senseless universe having galaxies, including the suns, as all unconscious; a mechanistic doctrine laid in place in the 1700s by René Descartes. In the twentieth century, James Lovelock and Lynn Margulis definitively broke this mechanistic mold with the "Gaia theory," the idea that earth is a self-regulating system, an organism. This opens to the idea of consciousness in the whole cosmos.

Sheldrake takes on the idea of cosmic consciousness directly when he says:

> But if the universe is more like an organism than a machine, then so is our galaxy and so is our sun. The sun has highly complex patterns of electromagnetic activity within it and on its surface. Its patterns of activity are much vaster and more complex than the electromagnetic activity in our brains. Most scientists believe that the electromagnetic activity in our brains is the interface between body and mind. Likewise, the complex electromagnetic activity in and around the sun could be the interface between its body and its mind.
>
> (Science and Spiritual Practices, 87)

Why couldn't the sun have a mind, he wonders? Why wouldn't the energetic solar body at the center of our planetary circling send out emissions that track us as we whirl around? Sun sends out light, and also permeates our solar system with solar wind, energetic streams of particles. And just as the physical activity of our brains' electrical output is measurable, so could the sun's consciousness be measurable as well? And if measurement is one way of knowing, then perhaps the sun's consciousness is knowable as well.

Microbia

Microbes are the greatest chemical inventors in the history of the earth . . .
From the early atmosphere of the young Earth . . . bacteria . . . removed the
carbon dioxide and produced oxygen. Bacteria truly have made the planetary
atmosphere what it is today.

    —Lynn Margulis and Dorion Sagan, *What Is Life?*

Microbes, as described by Lynn Margulis and Dorion Sagan, are tiny
life beings who discovered how to trap time and space within cell walls,
using the chemistry of metabolism to keep the past alive into the present,
passing it on through reproduction and DNA communication among
each other. They are our most faithful historians.

The hypothesis of Lynn Margulis is that life is a matrix of micro-
biota who developed cellular walls and metabolism using air, sun and
water, and who appear to have developed larger organisms—organ by
organ—that ultimately led to plants, animals, and us. Their metabolic
processes developed the atmosphere and much of the mineral rich earth
floor that supports all of us. We live in their world, and they permeate
us. They are our ancestors.

A single bacterial cell can survive essentially forever in its original form, as generation after generation bacterial copies of itself are made by cell division. (*What Is Life?*, 91)

Microbes have evolved over the face of the earth into scads of different varieties, from tiny fungi who lead tree roots to water in the soil, to colonies that oxidize iron, in the past created oxygen (by separating the O2 from the H in water) and which have evolved into increasingly complex colonies of cooperation, leading to complex functional organs and then complicated creatures. They not only inhabit us, they *are* us. They contribute at least as much DNA to each cell as our parents did. They are present to assist the egg's implantation in the uterine wall. They inhabit the pregnant uterus, co-creating the pregnancy; the fetus becomes inhabited by its own unique colonies.

Every individual has a microbial print, as unique as a fingerprint; we breathe it out with every exhale of our bodies.

When I say "my body" whose body am I talking about? At the cellular level, "our body" or even "our bodies" is more accurate. My inherited cells plus more than an equal number of microbes, all coexisting, exchanging DNA information and contributing to my existence. To our collective existence. Some mass of me are brain cells. Some mass of me are microbes, distributed through my cells and blood stream. Microbes gather in my glands, where hormones course affecting my emotional feelings and responses. They gather in my gut, communicating with my brain about my metabolic being.

Microbes communicate through the exchange of DNA, which they do continually. Margulis and Sagan describe the process:

Imagine that in a coffee house you brush up against a guy with green hair. In so doing, you acquire that part of his genetic endowment, along with a few more novel items. Not only can you now transmit the gene for green hair to your children, but you yourself leave the coffeehouse with green hair. Bacteria indulge in this sort of casual, quick gene acquisition all the time. (*What is Life?*, 93)

And because of this gene exchange capacity, Margulis concluded that the earth's bacteria constitute a single species.

I call this net of life 'Microbia,' not only because I like the sound of the word, but as an appropriate name for a contemporary goddess/god of life, one that has been identified in laboratories, engaged with microscopes and chemicals, and continues to be described as primary to life on earth.

> Today the low regard for bacteria as Lilliputian 'agents of disease' still obscures their enormous importance to the well-being of all the rest of life. (*What is Life?*, 88)

Antonie van Leeuwenhoek of Holland (1632–1723) improved the grinding of lenses and peering through them discovered a tiny new world. He saw bacteria, yeast, blood cells, and miniscule animals swimming in drops of water. The human view of "life" began to change and continues changing as science refines the capacity of microscopes to detect tinier and tinier life forms, some living miles under the surface of the earth.

When first viewed through the earliest microscopic lens the initial encounters with microbes changed medicine's view of illness. As research began, the minute beings came to be identified as enemies, something that "invaded" and "caused" debilitating, often lethal, illness. But now microbiologists have become far more sophisticated, both instrumentally and philosophically, in understanding microbes as the primal matrix of all life, though popular understanding is only slowly catching up.

The tiny ones are the elemental forms of life, and they created the terms and substances of our life: they created photosynthesis and oxygen; plants and soil. Their metabolic processes are credited with altering the forms of over one hundred minerals, including making iron oxides, and even creating deposits of gold from toxic ions. Microbes metabolize more creatively than anyone. The soil that grows plants, as well as the plant forms themselves, are their creation, Microbes tend the plants, as filaments of fungi trade liquid soil mineral foods for plant sugar, in a bargain swap that takes place at root tips. Fungi guide the root tips toward water. Hemoglobin precedes and supports animal life forms, and is a microbial creation. The microbes are the reason we have blood. And that we exist. They underpin the matrix of life on earth.

> Evolution is no linear family tree but change in the single, multidimensional being that has grown now to cover the entire surface of the Earth. This planet-sized being, sensitive from the beginning, has become more expansive and self-reflexive . . . (*What is Life?*, 93)

When I was twenty-one I went through about a year of medical laboratory training, becoming a medical lab technician for a while. I learned that gram stain is a particular test run in medical labs to help identify the bacterial cause of illnesses. Gram positive bacteria have skin that absorbs the purple dye; gram negative bacteria do not absorb it and instead will pick up a pink or red hue. The stain is done on a glass slide; the technique as I recall it, is to put a drop of the patient's blood or other fluid in the center of the glass, then use a second slide to spread the blood or swabbed fluid, as thinly as possible over the surface. The stain is applied to this thin layer along with fixing agents and then when ready the slide is examined under a microscope. I loved my job of looking into bits of the microbial world through a microscope, mechanical counter in one hand, counting white cells or bacteria among the red blood cells.

I had good personal reasons to take an interest in bacteria-caused illness. I had lots of sore throats over the years, from various conditions, flu, sinus infections, nosebleeds. It must be the salt content of the blood that makes nosebleeds so painful to throat tissue. I would let the blood flow outside until the idea of bleeding to death would lead me to swallow the blood, to keep it inside (had some idea that it would recycle). Then the pain, unbearable, so let the blood flow. Again, the sensations of raw, inflamed throat, swallowing something salty, panicked about dying. Feeling ghastly-alone.

By the way—though I had every infection that came down the pipe, even exposure to rabies and mild polio and treatable tuberculosis—I never thought, and never have thought of myself as "sickly" or weak. Always a warrior, an athlete, a champion. I felt sorry for Robert Louis Stevenson lying in bed sick as a child, and Elizabeth Barrett Browning suffering severe spinal pain and probable tuberculosis, and my favorite poet Edgar Allen Poe drinking himself into a fatal pneumonia. Never thought of myself in terms of the empathy I gave to them. I was constantly the victor, overcoming, getting out of bed renewed. Soldiers soldier on. So do poets, even while lying in bed wracked with some distraction. Poets make use of fevers and pain to reach for new images and ideas. Ancestral poets probably felt similarly about being champions, running Olympic races toward the finished poem or book.

Supplied with enough medical education to acquire a steady job running lab tests for a doctor, I could now go to college. Though my primary ambition was to "be a poet," I studied sociology to find out more about people. I thought I would become a sociologist, conducting research, formulating theoretical positions. However, I dropped out of school when the dean informed me that women could become social workers, but not theorists. (This was 1965, prior to the women's movement). I became depressed, not knowing where to turn. A few months later I suddenly collapsed with encephalitis and was rushed to the hospital in a coma, with seizures. The illness left me with some speech and vocabulary problems, that were minor compared to how much confidence I now had. No longer afraid of anything, I jumped off the nearest cliff called "Poet" and never looked back. Life somehow had made my turn for me.

My encephalitis episode taught me that an illness can bring about a positive transformation. Of course, the opposite can also be true, but in this particular case, the aftermath of my coma was a clear life path that I had been longing to take.

The encephalitis reset my life, as clearly as if it had been done deliberately, at exactly the right moment, and in response to my feeling completely at sea without a boat. Yet, it could have been coincidental. But other worldviews don't see "coincidence" or even the general sense of "illness" in such life-changing events.

My four visits to South India have exposed me to this different (to me) set of ideas.

> Mariamma and other village goddesses can take literally any creature's form, and deliver a message to you. . . . (Mahalakshmi Gangadharan, Ritualist, personal conversation)

The goddesses of South India, including the ubiquitous Kali, while experienced by devotees as loving mothers, protectors, boundary markers, healers, and much more, are not omnipotent. Neither are the gods, as they all fill different roles in the cycles of life, death, and reincarnation, and in being either active or reflective, but not both. This is in keeping with the ever-changing, paradoxical and collaborative evolution that describes life. In that vein, illnesses that are not necessarily tragic, and that convey greater meaning such as a major change in one's life, belong to the village goddesses.

Each deity is unique to each village, and they were still called "smallpox goddesses" when I was there in 1997, a trip made possible by my friend, Dianne E. Jenett, who makes a pilgrimage every year. Though smallpox itself had been eradicated some fifty years before. I was intrigued that the village goddesses of India were still called "smallpox goddesses," and their rituals are often associated with healing, especially of infectious, animal-borne illnesses. The goddess of each village is far more complex than this reductive description of course. The village itself is her body, the most striking image being portrayed by her head, placed in a sacred manner on the ground, just her clay sculpted or bronze cast head, on the earth. The villagers literally live with her, dig their wells and ditches inside her, plant coconut and jackfruit trees in her flesh. As a poet I found the image of her beautiful head on the ground irresistible. It made me both laugh and cry. I tried to imagine living every day with that sense of the earth as a living being.

Two things struck me in particular about the village goddesses. One was their consistent connection to smallpox and other infectious illnesses that have visible marks on the skin. The other was rain, often intricately bound into their rituals; rain shower that was expected to follow the completion of a ritual "within three days," people said. I witnessed three such public events and the rain shower showed up, as predicted.

When I first visited South India in 1997, my traveling mentor and I stayed with a farming family near the north coast of the state of Kerala. Our generous hostess was a woman about forty-five, who had been afflicted with smallpox as a child, sometime before its eradication. Her face was heavily pitted with the marks of the illness, a reminder of how serious this ailment was.

Village goddesses, intricately associated with infectious illness, can also be overwhelmed by it. The goddess can be the smallpox itself; she can give the smallpox or take it upon herself when it overflows the bounds of suffering humanity; and she can cure it. But as one researcher said, "Ma is not omnipotent, she can't do everything or solve every problem. She does her best."

The *meaning* of the illness, its significance to the person's life, whether good or bad, cannot be known until afterward, Dianne learned, as she told women she knew in a village in Kerala that upon going home after one trip to their farm, she had come down with chicken pox, which is not life-threatening but nevertheless debilitating.

"Then what happened?" they asked her.

"Then what happened? What do you mean?"

"Yes," they said, "what happened afterward? Did you change your life, did you get a new job?"

She thought for a moment. "Actually, yes, I did get a new job. One I liked better."

"There you see," they said. The gift of the goddess might be fatal or harmful, or it might be beneficial, a good turn in one's road.

Vaccinations have made village-based solutions to infectious disease such as smallpox less necessary, though when women make offerings to goddess by cooking a sacred porridge, called "Pongala," some continue to tout the smoke and intense heat as a curative or preventative. A role of the temple continues to be that of social mediator, as the smallpox goddess serves as a mirror of human experience functioning in part to prevent panic and encourage compassion toward victims of illness. If the goddess herself has given the disease, and has taken it on herself, and can in many cases heal it—then victims of the illness are not marked unworthy beings, rather they embody her divinity in some way, and are under her wing.

This discussion reminded me that smallpox has been a big player in my own family. My mother's face and body too bore pitted scars, though not very many. She had contracted the disease at birth, as the attending physician, who arrived to attend my grandmother's childbed in Kansas by horse and carriage in those long-forgotten days of 1903, had come directly from a smallpox patient, and passed the microbes to the newborn babe. She lived through this first ordeal; however, her scars were mostly internal, a time bomb in her nervous system. As a young adult in her early twenties that bomb went off, and she suddenly changed from a lively, engaged, ambitious woman to a fearful, paranoid person distracted with voices, visions, and powerful emotions beyond her control. She had some form of schizophrenia, though she was more or less functional between episodes, and eventually even held a job for several years. Her illness was one of a number of family secrets (and that's what I want to discuss—the role of microbes in keeping secrets).

Streptococcus pyogenes, which are also called group A *Streptococcus* or group A strep, cause acute pharyngitis known as strep throat. (Centers for Disease Control and Prevention)

Whether they get sick or not, as many as 40 percent of children may carry *streptococcus pyogenes.* (Does it really have the word "cock" in the middle of it?) Actually no. Streptococcus literally means something like "string of berries," and under a microscope because they are gram-positive they resemble pretty strands of purple beads. I wore them around my throat at times.

Starting with sore throats and then a tonsillectomy in 1945, and counting fourteen bouts of strep throat that ended in 1986, and not counting numerous other kinds of bronchial and more minor throat ailments, forty years divided by, say, fifteen major throat episodes involving pain, swelling, and fear of dying, the math says an average of one such serious illness every two and a half years. They were not regular like this; some were more humiliating or scary than others, as with a misdiagnosis (despite my protests) or a time the doctor's lifesaving pain-subsiding prescriptive writing was illegible. So return trip, try to find him in hospital maze. Weekend, he's off. Oh when oh when oh when. Will this ever end.

String of beads had ways of getting my attention. Waiting in emergency rooms, barely able to stand, clutching the precious piece of paper, then the priceless bottle. Gobbling the antibiotic like food in famine, food that was instructing the strep family to lay off. And they did. They rolled over, let the leucocytes claim their bodies, slunk off to some cellular hiding place. Waited. Bided their time. Reproduced, ate, excreted, exchanged DNA. Until instructions came through again. It's time: increase your numbers, get in formation. Go for the throat.

My mother had little capacity to take care of infants and young children; she abandoned much of my caretaking to my two angry, adolescent siblings, who themselves had been badly raised. When I was little my sister took me places, even on dates. "Having you there kept the boys off me," she said. When she married, she disconnected from me.

Ten years old when I was born, my brother was both my greatest tormentor and someone I looked to for attention. My brother, who had so many fascinating tools. A long sharp knife, boots with metal buckles, a motorcycle, the air gun with which he shot little birds, bringing them home for my mother and I to coo over and "nurse" in a bizarre and cruel ongoing drama.

As his sexuality matured, I was an easy receptacle for practice. My brother's transgression of my body, though probably not confined to one area, concentrated on oral rape, beginning when I was three years old and lasting until he left home when I was six. His acts needed to be kept secret, as he made clear at the time. I also must have known early on that my mother was not interested in any criticism of him. Decades later, in a fit of selfish self-protection, and no doubt after she had watched television programs like Oprah and Dr. Phil in which women openly talked about childhood sexual abuse, she suddenly said to me, out of the blue, "Whatever your brother did to you, I don't want to hear about it."

So no one in the family wanted or had ever wanted to know, and I did not tell them. I did not tell myself, either; I "forgot."

'Choice,' 'discrimination,' 'memory,' 'learning,' 'instinct,' 'judgment,' and 'adaptation' are words we normally identify with higher mental processes. Yet, in a sense, a bacterium can be said to have each of these properties . . . (Daniel Koshland Jr., quoted in *What Is Life?*, 219).

Sigmund Freud was first to effectively describe for modern people levels of mind "below" consciousness. The unconscious, he said, was the site of events "repressed" into forgetfulness, mechanics of function too habitual to need conscious direction, but also events too shameful or traumatic to be recognized or spoken. The place of this lockdown was presumably the brain. The way it has been imagined is through drawings of a mountain sitting in an ocean, just the top part of the mountain visible above the water of forgetfulness. My own sense of unconscious was always of a dark, empty though emotionally volatile or alternatively, numb, space, a cavern maybe, "somewhere inside."

This "site" or level did not keep its secrets completely buried. In me, it actually seemed to have an irrepressible urge to reveal; I just couldn't or was not ready to read the code. The strep throat illness replicated the sensations of what my brother had done: extreme pain in the throat, muscle aches in other places, sense of suffocating, choking, and being on the verge of dying, extreme heat and despair coupled with a kind of fatalistic apathy. It's as though the string of bead-shaped microbes were re-enacting the dramatic events stored in memory, complete with details, a kind of reality play for my benefit, and as though asking, "Now are you able to remember?"

Each bout of strep was accompanied by frenzied activity by people around me to rescue me, get me to an emergency room for a doctor's examination and throat swab, rushing to the pharmacy, my nearly fainting, moaning self in tow, to get the prescription filled, and then the lifesaving pills beginning their magical comeback dance. The entire episode lasted about a week each time. And recalling this, no wonder I never wanted to live alone.

My mother had told me that prior to the development of penicillin children died of strep infections, and that she herself knew of a boy who lived in their Chicago apartments, who had died of it in the 1930s. Whether that story was true or not, I believed it. I also knew that my first lover, Yvonne, had endured strep as a young child that left her with a rheumatic heart condition, whose recurrence was the direct physical cause of her death at the age of thirty-five.

Were the microbes just playing some game with me? My emotions as a child would have been so powerful, "This is awful," and "No one must know about it."

Even now, writing about it, I fear I will jostle something, and the strep will erupt. Strep has been a silent monster stalking me, striking at unpredictable times. The idea is so wrong that little children don't remember what is done to them, that the perp can simply say, "Forget, and never tell." Following the event with its high feelings, the microbes and cells remember. They have deep memory, buried in tissue and nerve, carried in the tiniest of packets. Relentlessly trying to tell their truths.

Life is matter that chooses. Each living being, Samuel Butler argued, responds sentiently to a changing environment and tries during its life to alter itself.

(*What Is Life?*, 226)

Amazingly, transformatively, at age forty-six after a year of therapy, my long-buried memories surfaced. Among them were my brother's actions. I gave these memories public voice hesitantly, not only in the therapist's grief-saturated office. I told my partner, my friends, and finally my whole audience, building some of the phrases of remembrance into public performance and published work. Each little reference felt as though I was shouting something shameful at the top of my lungs. I worked some timid phrases into a play, hidden in lines spoken by a mythic character; I watched the play seven times, transfixed by the reflection of my inside self on a stage, witnessed by thousands of other eyes, however unknowingly.

The year of surfacing memory was 1986; I'd had my last strep episode a few months prior to this, and then, never again. For forty-two years I experienced tonsillitis and tonsillectomy, strep fourteen times, countless sporadic sore throats of various sources. Because I am eighty as I write, there is a long perspective and reason for confidence: thirty-four years have passed since the memory came into my consciousness, and nothing like the old illnesses has occurred. I cannot find any way to think of this as coincidence. I feel a strange, uneasy gratitude for my string of beads. They enabled me to retain a deeply disturbing family memory until it could be revealed in the safety of feminist talk therapy. And then, something told the beads, no more. Consciousness, including the subterranean one, is dialogue.

Thought, like life is matter and energy in flux . . . (*What Is Life?*, 233)

The microbes are like the superintendent in an apartment building, living out of sight in the basement, taking care of the furnace, lights, garbage, gas, water, plumbing . . . while the conscious sensory selves run up and down the stairs thinking they own the place—they inhabit; but the super is who makes it function. Knows where the bodies are buried, what bills need to be paid.

Thinking about microbes and consciousness—what if they captured time and space in their tiny capsules, and also consciousness free-floating in the cosmos? This would mean that everything that can be described as living, has consciousness caught within. And what if consciousness is a result of reflecting and being reflected, of dialogue?

What if the cells retain some method of comprehending bigger pictures? And within the context of a body, not only "processing information," but processing and retaining emotion as well, then collaborating and expressing on the body's papyrus? Using their chemical tools to enable complex messages written in flesh and feeling. "Your brother did this; it was a shameful family secret; you felt as though you were choking and dying."

Margulis called them "brainless bacteria," speaking of the relative simplicity of their structures. Yet they choose. They communicate. They exchange information. They affect in meaningful ways. And somehow the streptococcus showed up repeatedly to somaticize my family memory, and replicate it for me, experientially. They were an integral and essential part of the inner workings of my unconscious, ever-busy, DNA-exchanging cell bodies that were both keeping and revealing the secret.

> Literal definition of Consciousness: having joint or common knowledge with another from con (together) + scio (to know). (Spacedoutscientist.com. 2016/08/06)

Consciousness is a result of "knowing together" and therefore requires reflection between two or more beings. Perhaps the reason I could bring my memory to surface was the reflection of me that my therapist had initiated. Seen by another person who wanted to hear my story, the memory could reach my middle, everyday, sensory consciousness, and my unconscious, the body-based, mute-except-for-enactment microbes and cells holding the memory all those decades could let go of their burden. Each time the strings of beads threw themselves at my throat to produce an illness, they must have known, as a group, that my inevitable round of penicillin would wipe them out by the zillions. Or if it was not they who knew, *something* in that soup of cellular mind knew, and directed the repeated dramas. And the microbes collaborated. And reflected my earlier self to me.

Microbes have capacity to emit radio waves; bacteria communicate via electric impulses. Some marine bacteria can detect earth's magnetic field and orient themselves with an internal compass. They have a number of methods for their dialogues. Within us, they use "chemical quorums" to communicate as a group, sending chemical messages into the blood stream, and up the vagus nerve that stretches from gut to brainstem.

They form communities, they communicate across distances; they live in every extreme of hot and cold, in boiling thermal springs, in ice cores of glaciers; and their fossils have been found in the oldest rocks of earth's earliest formation. They live in cloud formations and other atmospheric places, and at least one species is capable of freezing atmospheric water at a lower temperature, and therefore can precipitate raindrops that return them, like an elevator, to earth. They can possibly, in other words, make it rain.

This has me thinking again about the village goddesses, and how they are credited with causing, curing, and catching certain infectious illnesses. And in turn, these are as likely to be a gift as a tragedy. I'm thinking of this capacity of theirs as possibly microbial, a matrix in touch with its village.

I'm also thinking of various goddess public rituals that are often accompanied, in the middle of the hot season, by predicted showers of rain. I'm wondering, since little sentient microbes live in clouds, ride raindrops to the ground and some are known to even trigger rain: Do certain microbes read signals of rainmaking, is there some ancient human indigenous communication with the invisible mantle of life?

The mountain of the unconscious below water except for its bright little peak sticking into the air is no longer my go-to image for what is inside me, gripping my unspeakable memories. Instead, I'm holding the sense of a lively group of cells, exchanging the latest news, passing my memories on through cell division, translating knowledge into enzymes of feeling, shooting packets into the vagus nerve or bloodstream for delivery to the brain—or, to the throat? Showing off their new green hair. Telling those string-of-bead-shaped ones, "Stay on vacation, we still don't need you. That tale's been told."

My new and truer picture of my own unconscious is cellular and alive, in dialogue, its components are cells, nerves, neurons, microbes, enzymes, all comprising memory, constantly archiving and in communication with feelings, thoughts, and speech patterns of conscious mind.

Touching Spirit

Thinking and being are the same thing.
—Lynn Margulis and Dorion Sagan, *What Is Life?*

"Spirit" means different things to different people, and has meant different things to me throughout my life.

To one of my lovers, spirit was simply vivacity of life on earth, having no relation to what she thought were superstitions about afterlife or sprites of the land or a psychic layer of connection. To another of my lovers, spirits were everywhere in visible form, as ghosts, demons at the window, sex-induced visions, friendly entities passing through, even possible deities.

To the teachers I have had who grew up in the complicated world of multiple deities that is South India, everything is sacred, and encounters with spirit and what my own culture thinks are examples of "supernatural" and "miraculous" and "coincidence" is instead the stuff of life. Encounters and entities are very specifically named, closely described, taken for granted, along with extraordinary physical capabilities that are attributed to natural, intelligent forces.

Attempting to describe my various encounters with aspects of what could be called, in general, spirit in nature, my consciousness of consciousness itself continues to want explanations. As with any relationship, the proof is in the pudding, the reality is in the details of experience. And, these relationships, however mysterious, or jarring, confirm my childhood sense of being connected to other lives, lives without bodies, yet on earth, in the air, and in the sky. My working definition of spirit is a disembodied, conscious entity that has connected with me in some perceivable way. An unembodied presence.

Even "unembodied" isn't quite right—the ghosts I've seen may be waves of some sort that translate into forms in our minds. Other visions— lights in the sky, little dark, rolling earth spirits—seem to possess visible, light-reflecting though insubstantial, bodies. My vocabulary founders. Scientists and science philosophers use a variety of (also unsatisfactory) imagery. Rupert Sheldrake's description of morphic resonance (*The Presence of the Past*) situates in the idea that atmosphere/space around ourselves and other creatures, retains memory. He critiques materialist science as having rigidified, faults it for a belief in immutable laws; reality is more malleable and interactive than that.

Fredrik Ullén has found that the thalamus gland regulates the amount of information that reaches the brain, and he postulates that creative brains are flooded with divergent ideas that present more choices. The thalamus acts as a kind of valve in other words, and too much openness produces both creativity and overwhelm; his research suggests an association also with schizophrenic states of confusion. Both these depictions—valves regulating flows of information into the brain, and Sheldrake's idea of memory capacity in the atmosphere, suggest to me "mind" as larger than the neurological network that lives inside a skull.

While psychism is experienced by a great many people it is not accepted by mainstream science; the research of Edwin May, Dean Radin, and others show consistent statistical evidence that extrasensory perception exists and can be tested in controlled circumstances. Despite his findings, May does not think the existence of psychism necessarily means that intelligence exists outside the body.

In general, the laboratory methods of science are not suitable for answering most paranormal questions. Anecdotes are therefore invaluable, especially if careful notes are taken, and stories are told with some kind of context. I've been careful to select mostly examples that include at least one other witness. I'm keenly aware of the power of imagination, and the difficulty people have recalling exact events in tense situations, such as a crime or car crash. I'm aware that I want the universe to be a warm fuzzy place full of interactive intelligence. So I take good notes and try to keep a critical eye on myself.

And I find it impossible from my own experience not to think of intelligence, intentional connection, messages, visitations from "the other side" of my physical being, as real. And why not, for the time being, call this "spirit"?

Sheldrake has suggested that, if the earth is an organism, then so is the solar system, and by extension the entire cosmos. The sun emits electromagnetic waves, just as our own brains emit electromagnetic waves detectable with EEG machines. Taking his supposition further, Sheldrake asks,

> "If the sun is conscious, why not all stars. And if the stars are conscious, then what about entire galaxies? Galaxies are complex electromagnetic systems, with vast electrical currents flowing through the plasma of the galactic arms, linked to magnetic lines of force millions of light years long. The galactic centre may be like the brain of the galaxy, and the stars like cells in the body of the galaxy. There may be a vast galactic mind, far exceeding the scope of our sun's more limited mind, with vast electromagnetic extensions of its activity passing through the spiral galactic arms." (*Science and Spiritual Practices*, 88)

In thinking about consciousness, my own as my best known-to-me example, the stories I have told so far exemplify three layers: my everyday consciousness is *sensory*, using the five senses to inform me about the present, about phenomena. My unconscious is *cellular*, as suggested in my piece "Microbia," a collaboration of fleshly cells including those of the interactive microbes that inhabit my physical being. The third layer of consciousness, "spirit," is describable in terms of *radiance*—mostly invisible waves or rays, detectable by an as yet mysterious "sixth sense" or what used to be called "second sight." Psychic practitioners have a vocabulary that includes clairvoyance, clairaudience, and clairsentience, suggesting parallel sense organs that extend beyond, far beyond, individual physicality.

My imagination was caught by Sheldrake's image of the sun's emission of sentient rays of light and solar winds. I now think of the sun as drenching us with its fiery mind, of earth's microbes and the plants they created, chewing on photon particles of the living mind of the sun. This certainly is not the first cosmic philosophy to describe "eating" as having multiple functions. However, sun rays are not around at night when so much psychic input and extraordinary creativity is likely to occur. What accounts for this? Perhaps rays of the sun's mind interfere with rays from other cosmic minds.

An intriguing new theory of dark fluid gives my poet's mind something to munch on, however speculative. Jamie Farnes and colleagues at Oxford University have published a model trying to account for the anomaly that astronomers struggle to explain: that the galaxies are spinning too fast to stay in place; something besides their own gravitational pull must be affecting them. Since Einstein astronomers have used the terms "dark matter" and "dark energy" to refer to the 95 percent of the cosmos that is not visible to us but is detectable by its effects on physical bodies. "Dark energy" refers to the force that keeps the entire shebang expanding. Farnes has merged the two, into one concept of "dark fluid," a force with negative gravity. Other elements of the universe have polarity, he argues: gravity has poles, batteries have positive and negative poles, computers work on a 0-1 system. Mutual sex in my experience requires some kind of bipolar charge. Why not think that dark fluid has negative gravity, surrounding and pushing galaxies to hold them in place? Yes, why not. I love the idea that something invisible yet real surrounds us, that our senses are limited and suitable for our life spans on earth, but not "all there is" by any means. That the space between physical objects in the sky is not empty; is a living fabric of some kind, or various kinds— an ocean of consciousness. Ancient peoples, our ancestors, had methods of accessing the currents and swirls of this consciousness. I think we who live in mass culture will access this again, by reaching out intentionally; meanwhile waves of that ocean seem to reach out toward us.

The Fylgja: My Family's Inherited Spirit

As a child I often heard my Scandinavia-born father talking out loud to himself in our tiny apartment, though I could not understand the words. Because my mother was so fearful, I imagined that he was talking about us, even threatening harm to us. Yet without thinking about it, I too developed a habit of speaking out loud to myself, "talking to the air," because it seemed a way of thinking, it seemed like a dialogue.

I talked out loud, not just to the air, also to the moon and stars, to particular trees, to bodies of water, especially water running in the big irrigation canal near my home, the canal called "Mother Ditch." But nothing talked back, and I longed for a connection to beings in nature that just wasn't happening.

When I was twenty-six I had a vision. The circumstances were that in March or April of 1966, I came down with encephalitis, and was in a coma for three days. I awakened unable to speak at first, and struggled to reclaim a vocabulary, but was able to sing and recite poetry. I was emotionally volatile but also extremely optimistic and courageous, up for anything. This illness changed the direction of my life, setting me on a course to fulfill what felt right as my destiny. First however, I had a vision.

In fall of that year, I had turned twenty-six, and had fallen in love with someone who did not seem to want me. In my unhappiness, and while I was walking in the high desert feeling extreme misery, I came upon a chrysalis, some sort of moth probably. The container hung from a mesquite bush like a Christmas tree ornament, lantern-shaped, deep green with gold dots along the sides. I had hardly ever seen anything so gorgeous. Immediately after this, I had a vision of a woman, squatting on a mesa, several hundred yards away. She had black hair, was dressed entirely in black, intently watching me. I was held by her presence for a time, and then she spoke.

Though she was far away, her words were up close and clear as a bell. "Just do your work and don't worry about anything else." This became a lifelong mantra. By "work" I felt she meant the creative work I came here to do: "useful" poetry, and philosophy. By "don't worry" I felt she meant that everything would fall in place if I just had patience. I took great courage from this. I continued practicing poetry, lived in an art colony for seven months, took a poetry class and writing workshop. And waited.

The woman I had fallen in love with came across country to get me, and within a couple of years the two of us founded a women's press and a social movement on the West Coast. By fall of 1969, three years after my vision of the woman in black, my work took off like a rocket, as the feminist and LGBT movements exploded into mass forces of social change around us and embraced what I was doing. I was driven forward by all this activity until 1973, when I acquired a slightly larger bedroom/workroom and began researching subjects beyond what I had been able to do with poetry. One evening, I had a second vision. A woman, again sitting but no longer shrouded in black, was across the room, ten feet away. She had red hair and was young. "I am Monica," she said. "I'm here to help you." Well, okay. That's nice. I didn't talk about her or to her, and though she showed up several times, I just sort of tucked her away. Thought I was very imaginative.

I continued my research for years, though sporadically, as events around me became tumultuous, and dangerously so. By 1977 I was exhausted and in ill health. I had forgotten all about "Monica." Then she showed up again.

In the hippie and LGBT cultures of California and other places—Seattle, upstate New York—a diviner is likely to approach and generously offer to give a person a psychic reading or other divinatory form of advice. These free insights have included handwriting analysis, palm reading, even a street corner astrological chart. Gloria Anzaldua did numerology on my name when I visited her at her home in SF. So it wasn't surprising or unusual that a woman named Raye Amour, who happened to be a spiritual teacher, spontaneously informed me that a spirit was in a photograph of me, and was "someone from the other side," trying to contact me, or as she said, "trying to get your attention." She showed me a recent photo of a very tired-looking me, in a book of interviews, *West Coast Women Writers*, and along the side of the picture stood a ghostly looking "face."

"It's standing sideways," I said doubtfully.

"Doesn't matter," Rae responded. "Space is different for them, they aren't held by gravity."

I hope that I thanked her even in my skepticism.

Not long after this I learned to use a pendulum to access my greater mind and to read my own aura. One I hadn't realized I had!

"Everyone does," said my new spiritual advisor, Paula Gunn Allen, with whom I was now living. Paula, who had been studying in the emergent American New Age spirituality movement for a couple of years, insisted that we don't do our writing or other creative work "by ourselves." Rather, we have a conglomerate of spirits who do it. She called these "a committee." She could not explain more of what she meant though her certainty was evident.

I had already encountered two women who used pendulums to diagnose. I had been impressed because both of them reported that I should be taking certain vitamin B supplements for my state of depletion and early menopause symptoms, and they were correct. So once I had the little amethyst crystal on a silver chain that Paula brought to me, and had established the signal meanings of its circular and back and forth swings, I named it Monique and asked, "Committee? Can you tell me their names? Their qualities?"

"Yes, yes, and yes," were the replies. Seven names spilled out, including hers, which she said had earlier been "Monica." I used the alphabet chips of a scrabble game to laboriously spell everything out. The names weren't in any order but I noticed that when she gave me some of their qualities, three were male names and three female, plus one was androgynous.

None of this made much sense, yet I was being given a beginning map of my spirit terrain. I had longed for this connection ever since I was a kid, and now I had direct access.

Monique especially if I have too much invested in a question, won't answer accurately every time. Sometimes she plays tricks; she won't help me find lost keys for instance, and will run me all over the house fruitlessly looking. She consistently lies about money matters.

But for the crucial questions pertaining to my research and creative work she has been steadfast, predictive, protective, and a best friend. Monique also has told me repeatedly that she will stay with me until 2023, and then she will leave, to be born as a human woman in France.

When I first learned to access her through the pendulum I was forty-two. During that decade I also learned that my father had lived his life with an inherited spirit. I was astonished by this, believing that everything to do with spirit had been historically suppressed in Scandinavia.

My father, born in Motala, Sweden in 1898, inherited a spirit with whom he conversed by talking aloud, "talking to the air." My parents kept this a secret, though of course I heard him talking "to himself" as I thought. As I said, in my ignorance I imagined he was plotting against my mother and me; later in his life as he grew hard of hearing he spoke more loudly and on one visit I realized he was talking as though conveying and confirming information, talking as you would to a friend. During this time, in my forties, I learned that people from his birth-area in Sweden were understood to be "eccentric," and likely to be wood-carvers, and "with inherited spirits." He was certainly both eccentric and a wood-carver, but what was this with "an inherited spirit??" What is that? Why didn't they tell me? When I asked about this my parents did not deny it and finally when I asked specifically my mother confirmed the spirit's existence, telling me that she and my father often conversed with the spirit, who sometimes sat on my father's chest at night, and gave him advice. "Not always good advice," my mother added. I'm sure his chronic drunkenness did not enhance the dialogue.

To my parents, spirit meant an entity from the "other side" or "out there" that would live with you and that you could communicate with, and who would give you advice and information, and was inherited. My mother called my father's spirit, "one of those people out there," with a gesture toward the sky. Now I realize that, through my father's line, I too inherited an advice-giving spirit.

As I've said, my father communicated with his inherited spirit by talking out loud when he was alone in a room. Without ever using the concept "spirit" to explain the habit, I work out some of my ideas by doing this too, pacing up and down talking out loud, asking questions and waving my hands as though in dialogue with another. I am also fortunate to have found a second way to access information and advice—I talk to my spirit (my "intuition") by using a pendulum, a small crystal suspended from a chain, held between thumb and forefinger to allow a free swing which can then be "read" for yes and no answers. Pendulum use for divination is related to dowsing; both use an implement that is an extension of the body.

My first encounter with this instrument for reading intelligent radiance was a woman chiropractor. After listening to my premenopausal symptoms she took me into a back room and hooked my heart area to an electrode device attached to a wooden jig from which hung a pendulum, on her desk about twelve feet away from me. Sitting with her back to me, she put various bottles and samples under the pendulum, letting my heart's energy respond to each one, to determine her prescription: three supplements, folic acid, B6, and calcium. My symptoms, which included irritated eyes, cleared the first week.

About five years later during an eye exam the allopathic medical doctor asked about eye irritation called "dry eye", a common symptom in menopause caused by what current researchers believe is an insufficient production of androgen hormones. When I told him I had solved it with folic acid, he called in two more doctors to hear my story, including all the details of the pendulum session. "All we have for this problem is eye drops," he said, "and they don't treat the underlying cause." The doctors said they were extremely interested in the folic acid solution "though of course we can't accept the method used to arrive at it." Within a couple of years I noticed that some allopathic healers were prescribing folic acid, so I assume they found an empiric method of testing.

When Paula Gunn Allen, with whom I was living at the time, suggested I try using a pendulum myself, I was delighted that the instrument worked for me (and has become a lifetime "friend"). She set up a test using ten cups with a number of beans (one through ten) underneath; she sent me out of the room while she scrambled the cups every which way. I held the pendulum over each cup and asked for a yes answer on the numbers, which I said out loud. "Does this cup have three? Four?" etc. The pendulum gave a yes signal correctly for each number of beans under each cup, and after a few cups I was asking only one question, which the pendulum confirmed. That and other kinds of tests told me I could act as a relatively accurate medium for myself and for Paula as well. And Monique never wanted to be tested again. Problems come up when I have a strong emotional stake in the outcome or am trying to show off for friends. Pendulum does not work for everyone; Paula could not get accurate responses, though she had other psychic capacities.

Pendulum Test

At first, I thought the kind of crystal was what mattered; soon however it became clear that any object that will swing on a string could be used. I began to think in terms of "radiance," simply liking the sound of the word better than the more traditional "radiesthesia," a term for dowsing coined by French priest Alex Bouly, derived from a combination of Latin words for radiation and perception. Pendulum dowsing is widely derided, yet even the military has utilized the art to locate enemy ships or weapon installations.

Some skeptics have claimed that the pendulum, with its swinging chain held between thumb and forefinger, is moved through the minute movements of small muscles in the digits, and not by nonmaterial subtle energy. Even if this is so, and the movements are directed through the "subconscious" (whatever *that* is), this doesn't explain my experience with the chiropractor and her heart electrode device.

Why does it matter to me whether "small muscle movements" or "radiance" from my eyes or aura are moving the pendulum? Because I'm looking for spirit, with the working definition *unembodied presence*. My small muscles are part of my body, presumably subject to my will, however unconsciously. Sometimes I think the pendulum is probably being moved by small muscles. But other times I think it's pure radiance, and in my aura. And "small muscles" does not explain my experience with the chiropractor, who had hooked the electrode to the area of my heart, and by a long cable that draped across the floor. I could not possibly have caused her pendulum, which I couldn't even see as she bent over it, to swing through small muscle movements. She was reading a radiant beat from my heart area.

To display whether Monique's movements (back and forth, left hand circle, right hand circle) are caused by something other than small muscles in my fingers, in 2015 I set up a small test of my own, of separating my fingers from direct contact with the pendulum's chain, while still using conductive material to convey an energetic wave to the chain. I've tested this procedure on three occasions, with a metal jig, a thick stiff wire bent like a rectangle with only three sides. I fixed the long sides, the "legs" of the jig to a wooden chair, then hung the pendulum as a light chain in the center of the horizontal top rod of the metal jig. Sitting in the chair, I gripped the metal jig lightly with thumb and forefinger near the bottom of its stiff legs. In this exercise, my hands are nowhere near the thin dangling chain containing the crystal bob. Although I tried several times, there was no way that my finger muscles could jiggle the frame in such a manner as to make the pendulum move in a circle, let alone make it stop and then reverse the circle. Yet when I had thumb and forefinger of each hand on the metal jig's legs, and asked the pendulum to make the circular motions, it did so. The swings were not as easy or strong as when I hold the chain directly, but definitely following my instructions. If this is an accurate test, and I performed it several times during each occasion, then no small muscle movements are involved, and it's more likely that the pendulum is affected by rays from my eyes, or within my extended mind, or aura. This is mind within nature, mind outside the neurological brain cage. A mind that diviners using all sorts of instruments—constellations in the sky, tarot cards, cowrie shells, I Ching coins, keys and bibles, tea leaves, palm reading, drops of blood, hair, and certain sensations in their own bodies—access along specific channels. Perhaps related to Rupert Sheldrake's idea of "morphic resonance" of air as a field containing memory; or of "radiance" and "radiesthesia—a reading of communicative waves. Philosopher Thomas Nagel has argued that science needs to expand its explorations to understand that *mind*, as well as matter and energy (force), is fundamental to nature. We are particles *and* waves, and we have intentionality.

Recently, thanks to the internet, and European pagans posting about their family traditions, I now know the formal name for the type of spirits my father and I inherited. Guardian spirits that accompany families (though only some members receive them) are called fylgjur "pronounced file-gyur". They attach as an individual fylgja, to one person, taking the visible form of either an animal, or a woman. They are guardians and will stay with their person all life long, unless they come to dislike the person in which case they will suddenly depart. The folk custom of leaving the door open for a bit when a guest is departing, serves to allow the guest's fylgja to follow the guest out and not be left behind.

It now makes sense to me that my fylgja took the form of a woman and began connecting with me when I was twenty-six and had my first vision of her. Addition of the pendulum as a method of access, has made her more than a guardian and advice-giver about health and other matters; in addition, she freely delivers insights about my writing and leads me to sources. As helpful spirits, fylgjur are like faeries, toms, elves, wights, and fetches in North European folk animistic traditions.

My fylgja has associated herself with my third eye, or to use the Hindu term, *ajra*, broadly understood as intuition. I know this because about eight years after Monique named my "committee" as who does my writing for me, it occurred to me to ask whether this group of seven names had anything to do with chakras, the Hindu system of seven major areas of the human body energy centers that access cosmic influence. "Of course!" she replied with an exceptionally wide swing. She then helped me line the seven up along with qualities she had earlier suggested: root (gardener); sex (a dark goddess); will (musician keeping the beat); heart (a golden goddess); throat (a poet); third eye (Monique); and at the crown, an androgynous figure. I don't pretend to understand any of this, just note it. They also rather neatly lined up as male/female, male/female, male/female, and then androgynous. This is congruent with the Indian description of kundalini energy as two strands, ida (female) and pingala (male), that weave through the body's seven energy centers. This weaving balances the polarities of the two.

Science and spirituality use different forms of literacy—the language of science is intentionally impersonal, meant to distance emotion from thought. Naming something a "spirit" *or* a "nonmaterial entity"; a "vision" *or* a "remote viewing"; "Shakti" *or* "electromagnetic energy of the cosmos," and saying "fire is a god" *or* "fire is combustion" is a difference between thinking holistically or in fragments, allowing emotional and empathic entanglements or striving for "purely rational" (and seriously disembodied) slices of thought. Each is valuable in its own way. Each has contributions to knowledge; each can fall off its own truth path into fantasy. But a major, important difference is in the absence of heart and relationship; and another is the equally important question of volition and consciousness: Shakti, fire gods, and spirit all are understood as beings with will and living presence; the term "combustion" can never acknowledge or encompass this. By definition combustion is a mindless chemical process occurring on a presumed dead, senseless planet. Yet science is spinning itself away from mechanistic thought, with such advances as the Gaia concept of Earth as a self-regulating organism.

For thousands of years people of India have named primordial cosmic energy Shakti, enormous vital power that is animating of and interdependent with the whole universe; personified as Female Divine energy, not only existence but also liberation, especially in the form of Kundalini Shakti, a psychospiritual force of transformation. Paired with the cool, observing, and containing Divine Masculine principle, Shiva, Shakti has volition, and is Goddess of all creation. The two together have positive and negative polarity. This is one way to name radiance, movement, energy, electrons, and also fire. Shakti has both fierce and subtle powers, as well as eroticism in all its magnetic irresistibility. Shakti is intelligent life force and (erotic) love, eros being the first aesthetic sense, according to the ancient Indian philosopher Bharata Muni.

Sex and radiance

My friend Betty De Shong Meador owns a beautiful, somewhat wild ranch in San Diego County, which humans share with coyotes, rattlesnakes, bobcats, and an occasional mountain lion. My spouse Kris and I spent many glorious hours at this ranch, drumming, watching families of wildlife, picking fuzzy flavorful sage, drinking wine and telling stories. One night the two of us, newly in love, crept out of the ranch house with a blanket and a notebook, and wended our way to a set of smooth stones near a pond that fills during the rainy season.

My spouse and I sprawled in each other's arms, lying out on a broad smooth stone, making love. Our purpose for being out there was to get high on sex, make some notes about it, and see what happened. The ranch buildings sit in the foothills of the "Mountain of Moon-Lit Rocks" where about two hundred years ago in its shadow native indigenous people spent their summers near the creek gathering acorns, grinding acorn meal in cupules carved through their efforts in the flat rocks near the water stream, just to the left of where we lay. Here on this smooth, well-used surface, still warm from the heat of day, is where we lay down to experience what the night might bring us. Some stone surfaces invite your body in, this was the feeling, of being held. The moonlit rocks of this territory are peppered with mica and crystal bits embedded in the schist. My notes of that night say that we heard the stones "singing."

We were stretched out on the rock surface in the dark when suddenly everything went still, all the insect, bird, and reptile voices of nature hushed for several minutes. We dozed lightly, then a sharp bright light came on us from directly overhead to the east, so close it seemed we could walk over and touch it—the full moon rising. We laughed in awe at how huge it was in this high air. Creature voices began to chatter and sing again. An owl came low directly overhead. Insect voices swelled like violins. I had just had a vision of my love as an owl warrior, painted red, black, and white. A bat shadowed off at a northward angle. The myriad creatures, night birds, snakes, lizards, grasshoppers, rustled and murmured in their course of earning a living, talking to each other, raising families. We continued making love.

After 2:00 a.m. and still in an altered state we decided to go back to the ranch house and stood up. We gathered the notebook, our blanket, a water bottle. Then we saw something unexplained and unforgettable.

"Look up," I said, my mouth gaping open. The western sky was one huge electric grid, shaped like a net—high in the sky, higher than aurora borealis I had seen as a child in Chicago and again, as a purple curtain in Vancouver, Washington. Those lights are thirty thousand feet high; this white net took up more of the sky than that, though stopping before reaching the zenith. The net was not like something computer-drawn, it had somewhat softer edges but was definitely made of white light, not clouds. Dozens of lines in a crisscross-regular pattern, unlike anything either of us had ever seen.

I asked my spouse recently what she recalled, how was it shaped? She said, "I sure do remember it—I had my period and we were out on the rocks with the most glorious sky overhead. It was a white-light grid high in the western sky and it bent in the sense that it went to the edges of the sky." (From north and south)

That amazing night we were shaky getting back to our room in the main house, still in altered states from the whole experience of seeing a net of light across the sky. We had to walk along a narrow ledge next to the fish pond; I stumbled and dropped the precious three-ringed notebook, in which we recorded our visions, into the water. Swept the book back out immediately madly brushing away the wetness. Giggling and lurching, trying to stay on the brick path toward the ranch house as we knew the rattlesnakes would be out prowling around at night in the grasses.

The notebook holds descriptions and a few drawings of visions we have seen and shared while making love. The examples include visions and energy forms coming into the mind of one of us and then passing over to the other one evidently on the radiance of our sexual arousal. On one occasion, one of us passed the sight of a bit of sunlight caught on the edge of the windowsill, to the other one. We took careful notes, even during arousal and immediately following orgasm. We stayed in orgasmic states for long periods of time, immediately recording what we saw while we were "there," that is, in a trance.

We noticed that when we had the same vision, for instance a copper-colored ring, we saw it from slightly different angles, as though the vision was on some kind of shared screen but seen uniquely by each of us. From our Sex Notebook: "This involves psychic vision, as we often see streams of energy passing between our two bodies in three different colors distinct colors—white, gold and blue. This form of sex does not often lead to orgasm but rather to a great deal of agitated moaning and shuddering. 'Stoned' phenomenon occurs." So we were playing with the intense energies flowing through and between us, arousing visions of mysterious figures, colorful rays, past life scenes, early childhood memories—often quite painful but held in our embrace—and achingly gorgeous sensations.

Lots of people of all descriptions have these kinds of ecstatic, aesthetically beautiful experiences in lovemaking. Seems worth noting that the clitoris is shaped like a dowsing instrument—penis is like a wand, while the clitoris is forked, has long wings (and two shorter plump wings) wrapped in nerves, flanking each side of the vagina. Not much of a jump to imagine these organs, in any combination, as instruments, like tuning forks, for engaging (conscious) radiance.

As for spirits, I always felt the ranch was thick with them, and that ancient faces peered from walls of stones. I took a photograph that seemed to show them; however, a well-meaning friend grew frightened of my talk of spirits and took the photo from me.

Rolling Earth Spirits

Thinking again of my recently learned ancestors' word for earth spirits, vaettur, I have seen some sort of unembodied presences on two occasions. The first occurred when I was riding in a car with Paula Gunn Allen, driving along a rural two lane highway (I think in New Mexico) one night, talking as we often did about out of the ordinary happenings, like a story we had recently heard from a mutual Cherokee friend claiming that time had accelerated by several hours on a road trip she made, and not just her experience of the time passing, but by her watch. I knew of people whose energies stop watches—but accelerate them? I have no reason to believe in physical teleportation, yet I believed she was telling her experience. I didn't know what to think.

"Then there are the spirits that inhabit the land," Paula continued. "They run along the roads. I see them sometimes. I know they must be real."

"What spirits are those?" I asked, thinking she meant visions of ghosts, or apparitions, which I had experienced more than once in the desert.

"*You know,*" she said (she often sounded as though I should already know this), "*spirits* that run along the roads."

"*What spirits,*" I demanded, looking intently out of the windshield into the night.

"Like *that,*" she said. And then, I saw them—four rolling beings crossing the road in front of our car. They were a little like black tumbleweeds, sort of matte black twine balls (but less dense, more airy) about two feet high, rolling along at a good speed, the pace of dogs or coyotes. But these were not live beings in any material sense. They had definite shapes yet were softer around the edges than tumbleweeds would have been. They came from the right, crossed rapidly in front of our car lights and disappeared into the night on the left hand side of the road.

"What are they?"

"I don't know," she said. "I just see them. I call them spirits."

Now, at least I could distinguish between a certain kind of "spirit"—perhaps an "elemental spirit"—and a ghost. I see "ghosts" usually to the left facing me, and as though with an inner eye, sometimes also accompanied by a feeling state. These road rollers were several yards to the right of our car, and seemed very present and real, not a vision, though also not seeming to have anything like a material body, and not at all in human, dog, or other creature shape.

So, speaking of seeing a ghost with an inner eye, I was driving along a desert highway one day when a man popped into the back seat. I could clearly sense and see him in the rear view mirror—a late middle-aged small man with black hair in khaki clothing, a Chicano or Native man. He was relaxed and smiling, as we talked inside my mind: "Why did you hop into the back seat of my car?" I asked him. "I just want to go for a little ride," he replied. "I do this now and then." He stayed for about eight miles, and then vanished.

This vision was exactly like others I had experienced—of a ghost cat coming into my house for instance, and also of an acquaintance who passed away and days later popped into my living room, seeming very confused. "Aren't we related?" she kept asking me. I kept telling her no, we're not related—and finally asked her to go away, which she did. In retrospect, maybe we were related, by marriage anyhow, as her last name was Sutherland and my great-great-grandmother in her third marriage married a man named Sutherland. If anything like this were to happen again, I hope I would ask the ghost what I might do for her, what did she really want? These kinds of visions are rare for me, and not always full-body, maybe just a face, and not at all frightening.

Also, my experiences of the appearances of ghosts are entirely different from the appearance of the dark beings rolling across the road. I saw them, or similar entities, again, about twenty years after that first time in the car with Paula. The second time was in Chile, where I had traveled in 2007 to give two presentations. A Conferencia had been arranged for me in Santiago; the other presentation was to be at a retreat center in the Andes Mountains. My hostess drove me to a theater in Santiago, pointed out the marquee over the door, which read in impressive letters: Judy Grahn Conferencia. I was deeply gratified to see intellectual work given such respect, and the event went very well; I had the support of my traveling companion Anya De Marie, who had translated my presentation into Spanish for the screen, and afterward a lively panel discussion enhanced what I had to say.

Two days later we were driven into the foothills of the Andes Mountains, to a retreat center, and an "escuela," a gathering of women from seven different countries, therapists, body-workers, belly dancers, midwives, a theologian, three Aymara activists who had come by bus from Peru—a grand gathering sponsored by women-centered activist nuns who had wanted the great Liberation Theology movement to go further toward women's rights. That night we stood outside in circle, and the Aymara women offered a coca leaf blessing for the gathering.

The following afternoon, my presentation, which was on metaformic consciousness, didn't begin smoothly. We had problems with the electricity, and the conversion plugs. The wind outside had whipped up, and I felt uneasy with it; the wind felt strange (I can't explain this) so I went outside and talked to it while the tech people struggled with the wall plugs. Should I not do this presentation? The wind seemed to tell me that all was well, that it was *with* me. When I went back inside it surged through the building, slamming a glass door and breaking a pane of glass. Women ran to sweep up the shards, though no one seemed upset by the broken glass. With that beginning I plunged into my talk, and to my great relief, people chimed in with their own examples, weaving my theoretical story into their own cultural knowledge. Judy Ress and Rachel Fitzgerald translated my English into Spanish, while the theologian Yvone Gibara translated the Spanish into Portuguese for the Brazilians.

A bowl of water I had left out on a table turned up spilled—a good sign as I had often heard from the Yoruba priestess Luisah Teish—she said that spilled water means the goddess has approved of the meeting. Following my presentation, which with all the intense interaction, went for over three hours, we all danced. As dusk fell, I gathered my materials, and began walking back to my room, a half-mile down the road. I was walking alone, not thinking about much of anything, feeling relieved and satisfied; then immediately to my right I saw them—three rolling matte-black tumbleweed-shaped spirits, gamboling down the side of the road as though to keep me company. They had the joyful, focused bouncing gait of dogs who run free, and I was delighted to see them. I smiled as I walked along. Just before a turn in the road that led directly to my motel room, they vanished to the right, off into the wilderness.

Precognition Warnings

So okay, some spirits wander the earth, and I'm happy that I got to see them. But it's our own spirits that we live with everyday, the intelligent radiance that permeates us, and that, as most people believe, lives on after our bodies die. That spirit has sight far beyond what ordinary eyes and other senses perceive. My friend Quin told me this story recently: In October of 2017, she and her husband were sleeping in their house in Santa Rosa; a little dog lived with them, but was in a veterinarian hospital that night, miles away, recovering from an operation. Quin woke because their dog was rapidly licking her face. She rose up thinking to take care of the animal, and found no dog; instead she found their house full of smoke. The ultra-destructive Tubb's Fire was upon them, and the two got out, along with tens of thousands of other evacuees, with just their pajamas. The dog, Quin believes, saved their lives with an urgent psychic message.

My own life was saved one day with what seems to me a spirit message. I was mindlessly steaming south on Highway Five toward Los Angeles, seventy miles an hour, head in the clouds, when I had a powerful sensation and vision of leaving my body, The vision was attention-getting; "I" became a kind of tornado-shaped, fog-colored wisp sucked off from my left side, out of my body, and out through the pane of the driver's window. The sensation was so alarming that I was completely alert and gripping the steering wheel when a couple of minutes later I spotted a box mattress in the middle of my lane, and was able to swerve into another lane just inches from hitting it. Evidently I had received a warning from some part of me that could see a few miles ahead.

Another precognition was more about time than space. One year I had repeated sensations of being rear-ended while driving around in my beloved Ford Maverick. This was the first car I had every bought and that was "mine." I paid $1,700 cash for what was love at first sight, a two-toned car that looked like an orange popsicle with its orange body and white roof. The car had no seatbelts (former owner took "maverick" seriously) and one tire fell off completely on Mission Street just blocks from the dealer's lot, where they could not believe their good fortune to have a four-minute sale from a sucker with cash. While I signed papers, they had rushed around changing okay tires for worse. The car was never able to cling to SF hills in the rain either, performing hair-raising backward slides downhill on slick trolley car tracks. But I didn't care. Car love is not explainable, it's like cat love.

Then one afternoon during the year of my repeated and nerve-wracking rear-ending precogs I was rear-ended on Telegraph Avenue. I was the last one hit in a three-car pile-up, and my body was mashed backward against the seat by the forward motion as my car was propelled into a crosswalk. Somehow my foot hammered the brake in time to not hit a young man on a bike that was falling over in front of my horrified eyes. He came to the window, pale and intense, to thank me for getting to that brake and not causing him serious injury or death. Orange popsicle was totaled, and I am left with a mystery: I have no doubt that my precogs saved the young man. But why, if my spirit guardian was being so diligent, didn't she just tell me to take another street? Why didn't some other spirit tell the young man not to cross yet? Or tell the driver of the speeding car something? This accident was "predicted" by my sensations months before it happened but why? No one has sent me an answer.

But some visitations seem more clear. Quite out of the blue I was able to act as a medium and give a suffering person emotional relief, through seeing a spirit clear as day, and as though speaking through an open window to someone from another plane.

A Window in the Air

Once, in 1985 I think, (while I was busy avoiding going to a therapist) answering an ad for a workshop on controlling one's emotions, in San Francisco, I stumbled into a group of people dressed strikingly in different shades of red. Around their necks, each wore a picture of their guru, Bhagwan Shri Rajneesh, mystic and religious leader of what later became a controversial movement in the US.

Curious, I stayed for their workshop and returned for two more sessions, even though some of the exercises were too extreme for me and left me depleted and ungrounded, because I didn't really need them. I was already plenty opened up, and if anything needed help closing some portals down. The exercises were breathing, yoga postures, and holding our palms out to physically feel the strength of another person's aura energy. This last was interesting to me because I found I could indeed feel someone from across a large room. Yet overall in the sessions, more of my energy was going out than coming in.

But for some unknown reason I just kept going back, a second time, then a third. In the last one I was paired with another visitor; we were to practice reading each other's auras. I was already irritated and skeptical, and now even more so as we were total strangers. I hoped we wouldn't be told to gaze into each other's eyes, as I dislike that kind of forced intimacy; I hoped we wouldn't sit awkwardly for minute after minute not knowing what to do.

Sitting cross-legged across from each other on a floor mat, following instructions we spoke a few sentences about ourselves. He was a very sad, defeated-looking middle-aged man, who told me that he was a journalist; he told me what SF paper he worked for. He said nothing more about himself. To my surprise I went into an altered state and immediately saw, as though a window opened in the air, the face and shoulders of a middle-aged woman, a little to my left, and directly next to his right shoulder. She had dark hair neatly combed, and I could see the top part of her blouse or dress. She looked at me somewhat urgently and instantly spoke, telling me to tell him that she loved him, would always love him, and that "everything is all right." When her image faded I told him what I had just seen and heard, describing what I could see of her dress, age, and appearance, and repeating her exact words.

I hoped he wouldn't think I was crazy or making something up; I was surprised that this had just happened. Instead, he broke into sobs, hands over his face, his shoulders shaking with his emotion. Then after a minute or two he threw his head back and began to smile and laugh aloud while rocking back and forth in what could only be interpreted as sheer joy. Tears continued to spill from his eyes, ran down his cheeks.

When he could speak he explained, "That's my wife. When she died we were estranged, things didn't get said, or the wrong things. I've been so guilty . . . but oh! She says it's okay, she isn't angry with me . . . this changes everything!" He clung to my hands expressing gratitude for a long time, and left the meeting with bright happy eyes and a light step, so different from the sad, slump-shouldered fellow I had met earlier. I don't recall if he tried to read *my* aura that day, because it didn't matter; it was clear to me that our meeting was so that I could have a vision, a visitation, from his wife, from the spirit of his wife, and deliver her crucial message to him. I was an agent of intervention for his anguished state of grief. I watched him walk with a vibrant step out the door, then I rolled up the mat and went home.

Like many another creature in this life on earth, I had been compelled by unknown forces to be of assistance to someone I did not know. She had popped into view right next to his shoulder, in his aura. We each have auras, that seems clear to me. Creatures must have them as well, some kind of consciousness that permeates and goes beyond their physical bodies, through which they convey and receive information, and even, as I did, instruction. Does the earth also have an aura?

Dark/Light Love Falling Out of the Sky

Science teaches that 95 percent of the universe is composed of dark matter and dark energy. James S. Farnes is an astrophysicist who recently has suggested that dark energy and dark matter combine into what he calls "dark fluid," an invisible substance with negative gravity. Dark matter is invisible because it neither absorbs nor reflects light, and its negative gravity pushes matter apart, thus holding physical bodies such as the stars, planets and suns of galaxies in place. "Unlike familiar positive mass matter, if a negative mass was pushed, it would accelerate toward you rather than away from you." He's arguing that polarization is a principle—of, as I said earlier, magnetism, (north and south) of electricity (positive and negative) and of computers (0/1). And, I would add, the cool/hot principles of Shiva and Shakti; also in Gay culture, the concept of butch/femme describes a necessary polarity for sexual attraction.

I'm remembering also that Paula taught that polarity is a feature of psychic or altered states of consciousness. The person or persons going into trance or receiving information will feel hot, and hyper-excited while some of those around him/her/them will feel cold and even sleepy. Once, in a trance session in which I felt cold and weak, she said I was serving as a kind of "battery" for the psychic trance state she was experiencing.

Ten years after this, I enrolled in a graduate program directed by Elinor Gadon, the feminist art historian and Indologist. The program was perfect for me; I had for fifteen years been certain I would someday earn a PhD. But I was also unbearably lonely. Most of the other students were middle class women from Christian backgrounds, heterosexual, of European descent like me, but I had long been alienated from this demographic, even from my own cousins.

Two years into the program, which met for a long weekend once a month at a sprawling ranch type house among hills coated in oak trees near Lafayette, California, something extraordinary happened. Class finished for the day, we'd had dinner; I had drunk two or three beers and wandered out onto a broad deck facing west. Venus was up so I began talking to her as I often do, expressing a grief I felt for old comrade poets I had known and loved, and who had passed on. I began pacing and a chant developed in which I named these women lost to me, and repeated "I miss you so much. I miss you so much."

Another student came out, one with some Native American ancestry, who had picked up on my distress. I sat down on one of the wooden steps, I was crying.

"I feel like screaming," I said.

"Go ahead and scream," K. said. "I'll hold you."

She sat down beside me and put her arms around my shoulders. I opened my mouth and cut loose to the skies. The most noise I'd ever made. The people inside came running out on about the third wail. Some gathered around me, touching me. One of them, a therapist, said, "Judy's having a regression."

I smelled beer from a bottle beside me tipping over. The porch with its long steps became a stage, as women, assured I was okay, sat down. They were looking at the sky, where something was happening. I was talking urgently, and feeling intense love. A woman who subsequently became my best friend, Dianne, was sobbing, hugging my legs. Our teacher Dorothy Ettling was on the other side, stroking my arm. Our teacher Elinor came out into an atmosphere that had changed. I was transfixed looking at the sky, where something I couldn't yet see was happening; I said I was feeling intense love, very very intense love.

"I want to feel that," Elinor said. She ran over to sit on the step down from mine, in between my knees.

As soon as she sat down I could *see* what was happening, a stream of smooth, thick syrup was pouring out of the sky, directly into my heart. The stream was about four inches wide, maybe more, and the color of dark maple syrup with amber highlights. It poured right through Elinor and into me. The feeling was absolute love. Elinor asked me to speak, and I tried, though it felt clumsy to talk, I was also gesturing to call others to come nearer to me so they could feel this and see the stream from the sky. But everyone seemed riveted in place. I was dimly aware that a deer was walking by in front of us. K.'s eyes were extremely bright, and she was smiling. I looked back to see women behind me sitting, staring at the sky, smiling. M. was standing, rocking back and forth. She looked beatific.

In an amount of time I could not say, probably a few minutes, maybe more, the dark syrup stream faded. We drifted inside.

Now I became completely rattled, embarrassed, obsessed that I must have been drunk, had drunk too much beer. But I'd only had three or four bottles over three hours. All the rest of that night I sat on Dianne's lap, weeping and moaning as a lifetime of loneliness engulfed my heart, while she comforted me. By morning, my alienation was over.

The impact of being in such a strong altered state lasted for days. Later, I interviewed, individually, the twelve women who had been on the porch with me.

Elinor, who had sat between my knees, face upturned to the sky, said she had never felt so much love in all her life. Neither had I.

P. and D. were transfixed by a peculiar streak of light across the sky, perpendicular to the dark syrup stream I was seeing. D. said she had seen such a streak of light before once, in her travels in Tibet. K felt intense love, "I have never felt so connected to anyone as I did in that moment— to you." She saw "leaps of white stuff that were like streams, crisscrossing between us." The "leaps" of light fell out of the sky three to five times, she recalled. She also felt a pulsating sensation in her heart area, as if it were opening and closing.

J. and L. kept looking at stars that were extremely bright. M., who had apparently gone into an ecstatic state, said the experience was "like being in a Kali temple" in India. R.E. saw very bright stars and felt intense love. Dianne said the stars looked exceptionally bright, similar to stars she had seen in Western Australia.

I asked, "How did you feel the next week following this event?"

Dianne replied, "In love with the world, disoriented, on fire, ecstatic."

Except for M. and me, no one saw the deer—an extraordinary thing, a group of thirteen women sitting ten to twenty feet from a deer, and almost no one seeing it, and those two who did see the deer, not mentioning it.

Then there was the temperature. April 13 was a balmy evening, not requiring even a light jacket. But P., who confirmed how balmy the evening had been, was now "freezing," during my episode.

She said, "I was shaking with cold," and she went inside to get a jacket. Dianne on the other hand was burning up, sweating.

K. said, "Sweat was pouring down my body, I couldn't believe that some people said they felt cold."

Seven of the thirteen of us reported feeling cold; another five, (including me) all directly in line with the beam of dark light that I saw, reported feeling hot. So, as with Paula's earlier "battery" example, our group experienced a polarity of heat and cold, evidently as the energy from the sky coursed through us.

From the women's responses I realized we had all been impacted, had all been inside some kind of altered state of consciousness that impacted us emotionally and physically, at least, if not also psychically. Interviewing those who were there helped me feel less crazy at the time.

What do you suppose we experienced that night? Indigenous traditions might explain in terms of ancestors. Yoruba allows for "affinity ancestors" meaning those you have loved but were not related to; this would certainly apply to my dear friends who had crossed over years prior to this event. They would have become my affinity ancestors and would certainly want to respond to my lonely cry. But could they, as spirits, gather that much energy and pour it down? Actually, knowing their power, I would say yes! Other explanations might drift into space alien or religious mythological territory, even to supposed influences of the planet Venus. But I am most intrigued by Jamie Farnes's new theory of the qualities of the cosmos that he has called "dark fluid" and that he described its quality so strikingly: when you push on it, it comes toward you.

Since Einstein, science has been aware that most of the cosmos is not visible yet has an effect on material bodies. The galaxies spin too fast, they should fly apart, so something besides their own gravity must be keeping them in place. That something has been termed "dark matter." Dark energy meanwhile has been supposed as the force keeping the cosmos expanding. By postulating "dark fluid," Farnes is describing a substance that has negative gravitational polarity, and cannot be seen, as it does not reflect nor absorb, light. It constitutes a "sea" in which material objects, galaxies, comets, stars, float. Galaxies, he speculates, are held in place by the negative fluid pushing against them, perhaps a "halo" of it forming around each galactic body, pressing it in place. So, wouldn't such a "halo" surround all the bodies being held in place?

Whether this particular cosmological theory holds up for any length of time, as a metaphor at least, it certainly helps me feel less crazy with respect to experiences I am calling "spirit." Something involving polarity affected all of us on that porch in the East Bay. And my sense after looking at the porch in the daylight is that the whole deck, though a pretty broad one, was much smaller than my nighttime memory; the porch had seemed very wide and the people farther apart than they possibly could have been. It's as though my consciousness had not expanded, but rather had contracted, had compressed, making the physical world seem larger.

The idea of consciousness in the cosmos as a "dark fluid" sea in which material objects float and are kept more or less in place and interactive through both positive and negative gravity forces, is an exciting one, (actually it's a calming one) and brings me back to thinking about Aldous Huxley's image of a "sea of consciousness." The ocean is not one single substance; it contains streams of various gasses and is subject to wind and tides. Regardless of whether we imagine I caught a tiny glimpse of "dark fluid" pouring toward my empty heart's need, what is immediately clear is that a stream, or more likely many streams, of *love* are present in the aura of the earth, and maybe the entire galaxy. And something, some sort of less-embodied presence that was visible to me and others, and palpable to many of those around me, poured a thick stream of that love directly down into my heart and onto all of us.

Farnes's idea is a beautiful metaphor to think about the cosmos as not just a scattering of cold, spinning rocks, dust clouds, and fiery stars, but rather a living field. I feel a sense of wholeness from thinking of "dark fluid" as, say, 95 percent of space. I like it better than being shot out of the cannon of Big Bang into cold emptiness. "Dark fluid" closes the image around Huxley's Ocean of Consciousness, and presents us as "held"—invisibly—snuggled between twin arms of positive gravity and negative gravity.

Aftermath

I have learned a new sense of self from writing the stories and accounts in this book. For example, people often ask me for my preference in pronouns. I have always said I am she, her, hers. But after this exploration of levels of consciousness, I have a new awareness that creeps into my speech, the levels I have identified as unconscious cellular mind, everyday sensory mind, and radiant mind (receiving from some "other" source, whether electromagnetic or something else). The pronouns that are appropriate for this sense of "me" as a "self" must surely be extended. The pronouns should be "we, us, ours." Reasons are:

1. An inherited Norse spirit accompanies and advises me, so I am not just one speaker.

2. I have a nonbinary sensibility that goes this way and that, so I am not just one gender, though I am one sex.

3. I understand that the microbes that accompany me contribute to my consciousness and continually interact with my birthright cells; my cells, microbial and bio, connect with my neurological system and are therefore part of my consciousness. I am not one entity, but multiple. We are hungry, we are depressed, we love life.

4. Consciousness is reflective; reality is created through relationship. When energy is witnessed and slowed it becomes matter. When matter is speeded up it becomes energy. Both contain information. The plural pro-

nouns are the most expressive of this interaction; communication creates relationship which creates reality. Therefore, it is appropriate to say, "How are we?" as an expression of this dynamic. I am the answer to "how am I?" in relation to who is asking or witnessing, so actually "I" am how *we* are. "I" alone is an illusion. We together create each other, not only through social formalities but also through the energies we emanate.

5. Rays from outside our body engage with our psyche and this varies from day to day, week to week, even hour to hour, down to milliseconds. Astrologers chart these emanations in relation to planets and stars, predicting feeling and mental states of curiosity, creativity, fear, anger, affection, eroticism, confusion, and more. We are impacted by rays that could be called spirit, or intuition, or a net of mind in nature, that enters in and engages. Again, "we" interact, the radiance impacts us, co-creating our state of being.

Perhaps some kind of metahumanism will grow from various movements, spiritual feminist, ecological, and transpersonal, connecting us more firmly with our plant-creature-stone neighbor beings, our resident inner beings, and our spirit beings.

Biographical Note

Judy Grahn is a poet, writer, teacher, and cultural theorist; foremother of feminist, Gay, and lesbian liberation movements and of the field of women's spirituality. Earlier nonfiction books include *Another Mother Tongue: Gay Words, Gay Worlds*, and *Blood, Bread, and Roses: How Menstruation Created the World*. Her memoir is *A Simple Revolution: The Making of an Activist Poet*. Two collections of her poetry, *love belongs to those who do the feeling* and *Hanging On Our Own Bones* from Red Hen Press, and also *The Judy Grahn Reader* from Aunt Lute Books, are available. In 2000, she received her Ph.D. from the California Institute of Integral Studies, where she is Distinguished Associated Professor. In 1996, The Judy Grahn Award for Lesbian Nonfiction was established by Publishing Triangle in New York; in 2016, the My Good Judy art and scholar residency was established in New Orleans. Grahn's work has been anthologized in collections from W. W. Norton & Company, Penguin Books, Penngrove, and Oxford University Press, among many others. She has received several lifetime achievement and foremother awards and has been Grand Marshall of two Gay Pride Parades. The Commonality Institute promotes her work overall, while a *Metaformia Journal* archive at www.metaformia.org retains articles on her Metaformic Theory. Her love of creatures and spirit is lifetime. She lives with her dyke spouse in Palo Alto, CA.